ION, 80%!

CE! STYLE

ASHION,

FIDENCE!

S 20% FA

80% CON

YOU KNOW YOU WANT IT

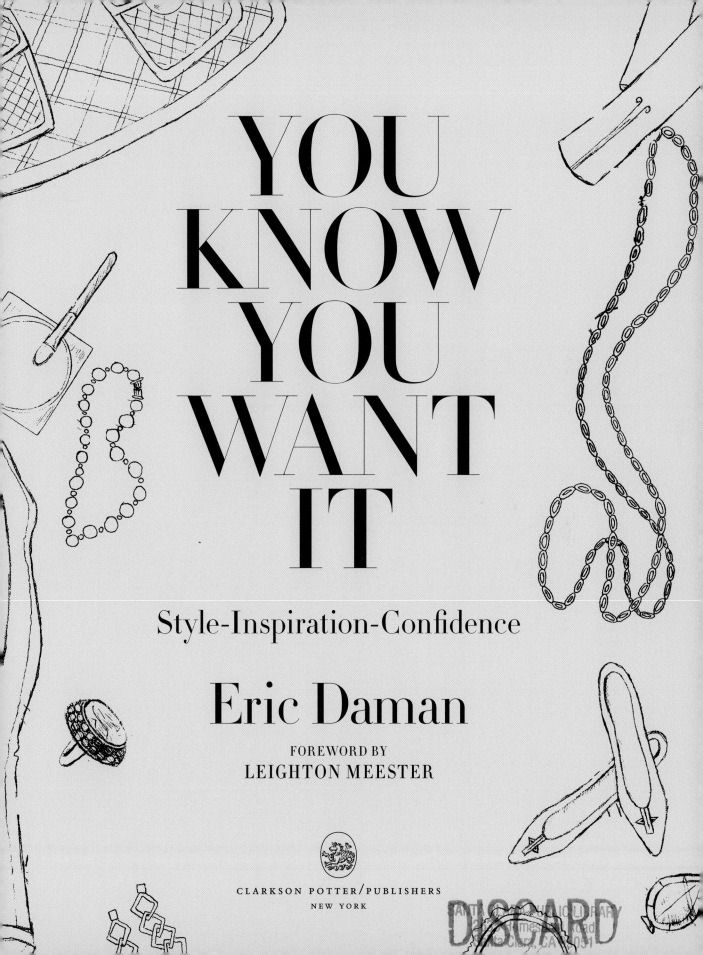

YOU KNOW YOU WANT IT

Style-Inspiration-Confidence

Eric Daman

FOREWORD BY
LEIGHTON MEESTER

CLARKSON POTTER/PUBLISHERS
NEW YORK

To my parents, who provide eternal
constructive criticism, support, and inspiration.
Thank you.

Copyright © 2009 by Eric Daman
Foreword copyright ©2009 by Leighton
Meester

All rights reserved.
Published in the United States by Clarkson
Potter/Publishers, an imprint of the Crown
Publishing Group, a division of Random House,
Inc., New York.
www.crownpublishing.com
www.clarksonpotter.com

CLARKSON POTTER is a trademark and
POTTER with colophon is a registered
trademark of Random House, Inc.

Library of Congress Cataloging-in-Publication
Data
Daman, Eric.
You know you want it / Eric Daman; foreword
by Leighton Meester.—1st ed.
p.   cm.
Includes index.
1. Fashion.   2. Grooming for girls.
3. Beauty, Personal.   I. Title.
GT511.D35   2009
391—dc22
2009029153

ISBN 978-0-307-46458-3

Printed in the United States of America

Design by Brian Lee Boyce and
Stephanie Huntwork
Image credits appear on page 206.

10 9 8 7 6 5 4 3 2 1

First Edition

Contents

FOREWORD BY Leighton Meester 6
INTRODUCTION Once Upon a Time 10

Basics

1. Spotlight on You 18
2. Want It, Need It, Have to Have It 30
3. Closet Case 86

Inspirations

4. Think Like a Stylist 98
5. Color Me Beautiful 106
6. Who Are You Today? 132

Style

7. Elements of Style 158
8. Rule Breakers 174

Maintenance

9. Behind the Seams 188

CONCLUSION Happily Ever After 200

ACKNOWLEDGMENTS 202
RESOURCES 203
CREDITS 206
INDEX 207

Foreword

When I first heard that Eric Daman was doing a book on style, I thought, "Of course. Of course he is." I mean, that just made so much sense. Because Eric is more than a stylist—he's also a psychologist, a scientist, and an artist. Simply put, he's a genius.

Imagine this: you're on set, in the middle of a frenzy of activity that would make the Energizer Bunny beg for a nap. You've had weeks of fittings and been in and out of different looks all day, done a month's worth of changes in an afternoon. You are getting sleeeeepy . . . the biggest cup of coffee in the world could not rouse you. But then Eric holds up a piece of clothing, a slip of silk dangling on a hanger, and whispers, "You know you want it." His tone hovers between sly and delighted, as if he knows he's about to make some kind of magic. And instead of exhaustion, you feel a glimmer of excitement. Because it's so true. You want it. You *need* it.

That's why this book will automatically go to the top of my reading pile. A handy, portable Eric Daman? It's like Santa got the note I left for him last December. I can't wait to own a repository of Eric's secrets.

I've worked with Eric for several years now, and having benefited from his advice both professionally and personally, I want to know what else he has to say, because he always has something fresh on the tip of his tongue: a new idea for wearing something more cleverly or making it even more darling than you ever thought

possible. And more *you* than you ever imagined. His approach to style affects the way I relate to my character on *Gossip Girl,* the wonderfully snarky and sophisticated Blair Waldorf, and it has changed the way I dress at home, in my real life.

When Eric dresses a character, the clothes aren't just an outfit. They're a statement. The characters on *Gossip Girl* have distinct histories, personalities, and outlooks, and their costumes are chosen to reflect what they're experiencing and feeling. Blair has a very specific style. She's got high-end taste and is always appropriately dressed. From the cut to the color palette, her look is all part of Eric's vision. He'll pull a shirt or a skirt or a dress off the rack, and I won't necessarily think, "Oh, that's so Blair." But once he accessorizes it with a scarf or jewelry, and puts it with just the right shoes and bag—it's spot-on. You might not have gone out and chosen it for yourself, but he knows it will work. And he can show you how and why. As soon as you try it on, you know he's right, plus you've picked up a little advice that you can use later in real life.

When it comes to the costumes, Eric is so well-connected to the character he's creating, the actor he's dressing, and to the clothes, that he can use any outfit to make a statement, make a point, and really strike a chord. I have to say, the way he dresses me for the shows helps me access and understand and create my character. Before I get dressed, I can know the lines and feel the energy. I'll go on set, we'll rehearse, we'll block out a scene we're doing, and I'll understand the motivations behind it. But the clothes add something extra, because the costume is so much a part of my character. Once I get my wardrobe on, suddenly there's a huge change, and I *become* the character. It's like slipping into another skin.

I consider myself so lucky to be able to work with Eric every day. I'm always excited when he comes to the set. It's a unique talent that he has, and a finely honed one. Styling is a science for him: he's just got such an amazing eye, and a wonderful sense of how clothing shows who an individual is. The psychology of it; the art of it—he truly loves clothes. Sometimes he'll refer to them in the feminine, as in, "She really needs a necklace." He isn't talking about the girl. He's talking about the dress.

Like I said, Eric is a genius. But you'll never hear him say so, because he's super-humble. That's the thing about him: he keeps his light under a bushel. So I'm glad that, thanks to this book, you'll all be able to spend some quality time with Eric Daman (and his style secrets).

Other things you might not know about Eric: He's kindhearted. He's a great friend. He's a risk-taker. He speaks French fluently. And he used to be a model. But mostly, he's just a pleasure to be around, and he makes the job fun. We all love fashion, but believe me, if you have a fitting every week, eventually, you kind of get over it. Somehow, Eric makes the boring parts amusing instead of (yawn). I love hanging out with him and going through magazines and jewelry and all the racks of clothing. He's the master of what he does. Everybody believes in him.

It helps that he's always so calm. I don't know how he doesn't get exhausted, because I get tired just wearing the clothes. Amid the crazy atmosphere of a television show, no matter what's happening around him, Eric has a very reassuring demeanor. I remember when we were shooting a prom episode, and the place was full of ball gowns just hanging everywhere, and everybody needed alterations and accessories. (There was a guard on set to watch the diamonds.) And in the middle of all that, there's Eric, just calmly tucking up hems and handing out glittering necklaces. *"She needs some more sparkle. . . ."*

In his own fashion, Eric is always extremely well put together, in a sort of thrown-together way. Perfect, but effortless. He's got his own keen sense of fashion that fits him. But he also has a way of translating style for other people that just really works. His approach is specific to the individual; that's what's so amazing. There's no one-size-fits-all with Eric. Everything is tailored, inspired, personal.

I've definitely taken some of that philosophy home with me. Before coming into the show and working with Eric, I was a more casual dresser. But now, because he's opened my eyes to all the different designers and trends and styles, I feel so much more comfortable going outside of myself and dressing up; I appreciate designer clothing and beautiful material.

Working with Eric has taught me how to dress more appropriately but also to take risks. It's a good balance, because I could never, in my own life, commit to one certain look. I can be brave and take on different styles. One day, I can be super-casual. And then the next day I can be dressed up, with a rocker edge. Or I can dress elegantly. It depends on my mood and how I want to translate it.

And when I need an extra shot of bravery, I just stand in front of my closet and imagine Eric holding a perfectly chic blouse out to me, whispering, "You know you want it. . . ."

—Leighton Meester

LOS ANGELES, 2009

ONCE
UPON A TIME

Paris changed my life. It might even have saved my life. It was a magical place with beautiful people draped in beautiful clothes everywhere you looked. Serious style was carried off with such a nonchalant air! A scarf here, a sweater over the shoulders there, and the woman who sells baguettes down the road is suddenly Brigitte Bardot in Godard's classic *Contempt*.

I learned that you don't need to be a movie star to look like one. That you don't need to go to prep school to dress as if you spend every summer sailing, you don't need to live in the suburbs to look like the girl next door, and you don't need to be an eighteenth-century vampire in

LOOKING GOOD IS ABOUT CONFIDENCE

order to accessorize with an air of mystery, romance, and danger. Sometimes all it takes is a pair of Repetto ballet flats with a vintage skirt and fishnets, a raffia tote overflowing with leeks, and suddenly you're a mademoiselle from Marseilles heading down to the pier to see what's come in on the boats today.

Paris taught me that looking good was about confidence. And the French *created* confidence, believe me. I feasted on culture and

PLEASE ALLOW ME TO INTRODUCE MYSELF....

savoir faire, discovered the nouvelle vague films starring Bardot, Anna Karina, and Jean Seberg, and fell in love with quiet, understated chic—and couture.

A job at a très chic boutique garnered me a pass to Paris fashion week, and access to the best parties and the best-dressed people in the world. A call from Steven Meisel's office got me to New York to be in a fashion shoot with Kate Moss. Now I was drowning in fashion: the best stylists, the best models, the best editors, the best photographers. Each taught me important lessons about personal style and individuality through clothing, and in this book, I am going to share these lessons with you.

We're going to discuss how important what we wear really is, how the world uses the way we dress to draw conclusions about us, and how to use all this knowledge to look our best. The key is that "best" means the way you see it, not the way the world has imagined it. What I want you to come to understand is that your own life, interests, dreams, and inspirations are the building blocks for your personal style—and harnessing your signature colors and pieces will be the trick to creating your own amazing look.

all of my *EXPERIENCES* have informed my *PERSONAL AESTHETIC*

All my experiences have informed my personal aesthetic, but when I am dressing my actors, I pay close attention to what is specific to their character and not just some blanket view of "fashion." Costume design is one of the essential ways that a character's personality and uniqueness are expressed. Clothing helps make the character original and identifiable, communicating who they are, what they do, where they live, what they want. Really, whether you realize it or not, costume design is what you do every time you get dressed.

1975: Feeding seagulls in Florida.

Your wardrobe should reflect what is essential to your lifestyle, location, and vocation. Are you a jet-setter or an at-home mom? Are you an Eskimo in an igloo or a Floridian floating in a pool? Are you a power broker or a temp? Your goal will be to develop a refined, cohesive style via a carefully collected array of options you can mix and match. Style should be fluid. While it can be comforting to establish a basic style persona that embodies who you are day to day, breaking out of that mold is highly recommended, not to mention a lot of fun. Your wardrobe should allow room for enough drama to keep you feeling innovative and original, with plenty of go-to basic essentials that empower your specific lifestyle.

As you continue your journey through this book, you will learn, as I have, how to create and perfect your own unique personal style. The trick to dressing well is to create a "costume closet" that will give you the tools to pull out the perfect ensemble for an early-morning meeting, a late night out dancing, or a weekend brunch recovering. We'll examine the pieces you have and figure out which pieces you need, which colors you should be wearing around your face, and which so-called figure "flaws" are actually the parts of your body you should be trying to accentuate.

You'll learn which investment purchases you need to look 100 percent fabulous (even when they're 50 percent off) and discover what trends to skip at the boutiques and save for a trip to Target. You'll discover the five basic fashion icons and use them as inspiration for your own particular style blend, adding touches like your "signature piece" to express your original point of view. Remember, why buy it if you can't *own* it?

no matter where you live, what you do, or how old you are, you can be a *FASHION FORCE TO BE RECKONED WITH*

Get ready for an entertaining educational expedition animated with insider tips, pretty pictures, and easy, breezy advice. And if you want to know where to pick up that perfect little dress, just flip to the resources.

Are you ready to take a chance, express your own unique style, and be the best you possible? I dare you!

—Eric Daman

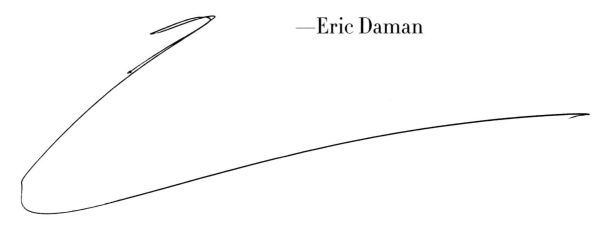

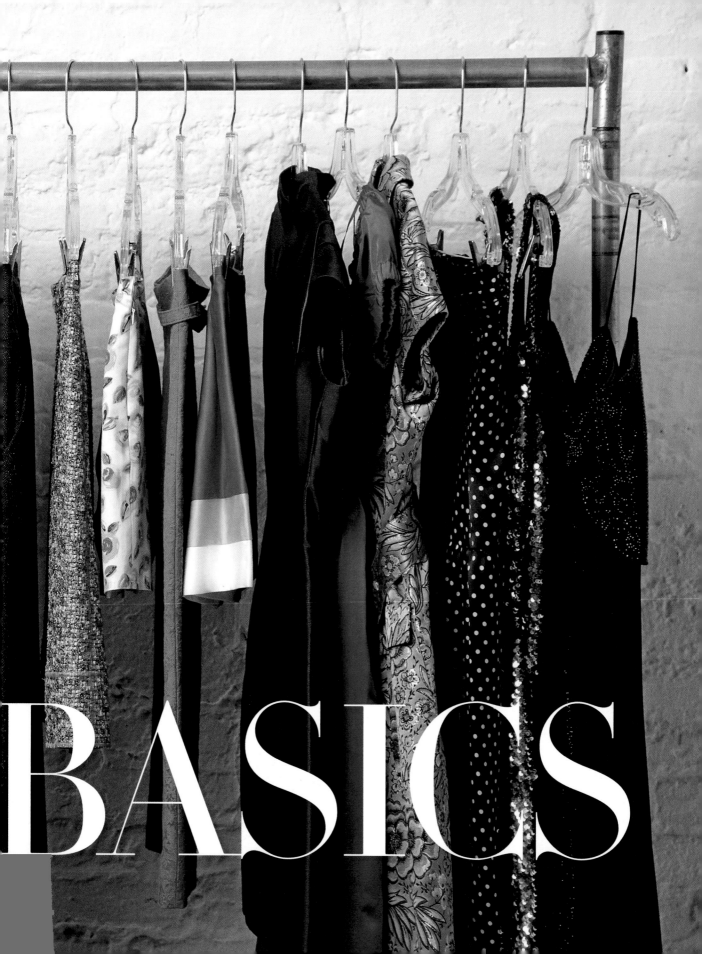

BASICS

1. SPOTLIGHT

24K CARROT
SAUCY APPLE

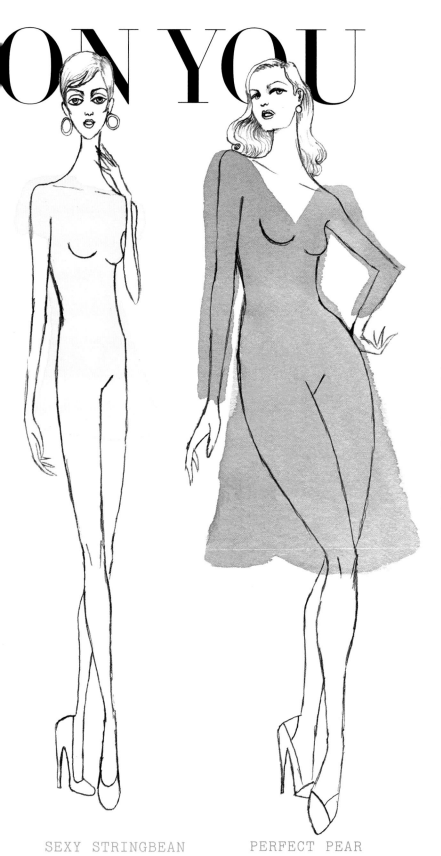

SEXY STRINGBEAN PERFECT PEAR

Hey, snowflake.

Ever notice that your curves and angles don't match up with your best friend's? That's because we're all different. In order to find your best silhouettes, in this chapter, you're going to take measure and discover your hidden treasures.

Take Measure

When you were born, one of the first things the doctor did was measure you from the tip of your tiny toes to the top of your sweet little head. It's time to get out the ruler again. This is the first step toward developing your signature style and choosing the most flattering shapes for your figure.

You'll need a tape measure, a pen and paper, and a trusted friend to take notes. You'll use the numbers to determine what figure category you fall into: *T-frame, I-frame, A-frame, or O-frame.*

Clothes that flatter matter: The cut and shape of a garment can have a certain magical power to create optical shape-enhancing illusions. Check out the following spreads for specific styles that will result in a sublimely seamless and impeccably refined look.

CARROT (T-FRAME): Shoulders measure more than hips.
WEAR: V-necks; tighter tops; fuller skirts; long patio dresses; wide leg trousers

STRINGBEAN (I-FRAME): Shoulder, waist, and hips are approximately equal.
WEAR: Boatnecks; horizontal stripes on top or bottom but not both; circle skirts; cigarette pants

PEAR (A-FRAME): Your shoulders are smaller than your hips.
WEAR: Halter tops; puff sleeves; A-line skirts; constructed trousers

APPLE (O-FRAME): Your waist measures more than your hips and shoulders.
WEAR: Plunging necklines; vertical stripes; darker colors; monotones

Discover Your *Body Type* in Just 4 Steps

1. LOCATE YOUR SHOULDERS
Measure from the outer edge of your left shoulder across your collarbone to the outer edge of your other shoulder.

2. BUST A MOVE To suitably support and effortlessly enhance your cherished décolleté: measure, under your arms, around the largest point of your bust. (See chapter 9 for more on underarchitecture.) Many women go through life wearing the wrong-size bra.

3. WAIST MANAGEMENT Old wives' tales locate the natural waist at your navel. Your waist is actually wherever your torso has the smallest circumference. Often, this will not be on the same line as your belly button.

4. HIPSTER TIPSTER Measure around the widest point of your hips.

Tops that top you off...

V-NECK
WITH A PUFF SLEEVE

A V-neck will lengthen your neck and streamline broad shoulders. A deep V makes your waist appear trimmer and minimizes a very large bust. A puff sleeve will fluff up scrawny arms. A wider sleeve will narrow your arms.

HALTER
WITH A HIGH NECK

The deep cut of the shoulder contrasts with the demure, high neck for a long, lean line that's more flattering for less-than-toned arms than a standard sleeveless cut. A halter works better if your hips are narrower.

BOATNECK
WITH A BRACELET SLEEVE

A boatneck balances out
wide hips and narrow
shoulders, making it an
ideal choice if you have
an I-frame. If you're
narrow all the way down,
the striped boatneck can
create a waistline where
none really exists.

CHEMISE
WITH A FRENCH CUFF

Everybody can wear a
chemise—and everybody
should. Leave it un-
buttoned if you like the
flair of a V-neck, or
button it up if you're
feeling a bit more
reserved.

CREW NECK
WITH A THREE-QUARTER
RAGLAN SLEEVE

The basic, go-to neck-
line. A wider crew is
better for a wider neck,
and a tighter crew for a
skinny neck. A three-
quarter sleeve covers up
untoned arms but still
shows off delicate
wrists.

SHORTS

A beauty who I work with
rocks shorts with tights
all winter long. So can
you—shorts are the new
pants. If you're wearing
shorts to the office, just
remember that they're short
pants, not long underwear.

CIGARETTE

I call this the "Audrey"
for obvious reasons. The
cigarette pant is as good
for you as cigarettes are
not. Slits on the side can
lengthen your look.

TROUSERS

A menswear-inspired pant-
turned-feminine classic,
trousers inspire confidence
and look great on most
bodies. Trousers should
hang low on your hips,
caress your derriere, and
barely brush the ground
over the back of your
favorite heels. (Hem them
to ¼ inch from the ground
to protect the fabric.)

Pants
that
make them
pant...

FLARE BOTTOMS

Forget Woodstock. These pants will look as if they walked off the runway into your closet (keep the flare narrower than 14 inches). Too much material weighs down petite girls, so leave these for your taller friends.

STRAIGHT-LEG

Like its denim counter-part, the straight-leg trouser is a fashion chameleon. Take it to your meeting paired with ballet flats and to dinner in heels. A pinstripe adds sophistication to your ensemble and length to your gams.

Skirting
the
issues...

PLEATED

Pleated skirts are great
for camouflaging a spare
tire or a butt that's
too big or small. Pleats
should lie flat. If they
pull, move on.

CIRCLE

The flirty circle skirt
still makes an appear-
ance on special occa-
sions. It does well at
dance parties as well as
at board meetings.

MINI

I love the mini, which
has a magnetism all its
own. It's a leg elonga-
tor and a curve-hugging
masterpiece. If you love
the mini but your body
doesn't, wear them only
in dark hues with opaque
tights in a similar tone.

A-LINE

This basic skirt style
is available everywhere.
Casual in khaki and
fabulous in a floral
faille, the A-line is
for everyone, and gets
an A+ for wider hips.

PENCIL

The pencil skirt works
for a whole array of
shapes, giving definition
to a smaller derriere
and shaping a larger
one. Try one with
fishnets (the smaller the
mesh, the sexier) and
slamming boots.

Know Your Lengths

HIGH THIGH

Stand up straight and let your arm drop to the side. The place where your middle finger ends is the top of your high thigh. This length is overtly sexy; tone it down with opaque tights or spice it up with textured hose.

MID-THIGH

This is the point where your thigh muscle dips into the midsection between knee and lower buttocks. This tricky length is best left to Julia Roberts in *Pretty Woman*.

ABOVE THE KNEE

One of the most seductive lengths; skirts should nestle just above the kneecap where there's a slight indent. Ideal for most shapes.

BELOW THE KNEE

Find the point where
your leg dips in above
your calf, and hem to
just above that dip,
highlighting it. Best if
feeling a bit more
demure.

MID-CALF

Your calf muscle tapers
mid-calf, pointing you
in the right direction.
This is the most
matronly of lengths;
keep it youthful with
great heels and light
fabrics.

ANKLE

This length can leave
men dreaming of the
lines lingering above.
Find the narrowest part
of your ankle and go up
1 inch.

2.
WANT IT, NEED IT, HAVE TO HAVE IT

Jeans for your genes

T-shirts fitted to a T

Sweater, singles or in sets

Cardigan borrowed from the ex

Suit suited for success

Chemise cut-to-please

Pants only if they enhance

Dress, perfect, little, not necessarily black

Shoes you'll be a shoe-in

Accessories sweeten up with arm candy

Be a
Jeanius!

It's as easy as
1. ignore the size
2. find your fit
3. define your style

Jeans

are a tried-and-true classic, dating back to the Wild Wild West when gunslingers, gold rushers, and Canadian tradesmen were all clad in the rugged, rigid Levi's of days past. Today's market is an overwhelming sea of deep indigo, sandblasted blues, and overembellished azure.... Ready to stop treading water and find your way back to shore?

your most DEMOCRATIC and ESSENTIAL piece

Ignore the Size

Size is usually your starting point; you've got to start somewhere. But remember that all brands are sized differently. Pay no attention to the number on the label, and do not despair if you must go a size up to find the perfect pair. Almost all women have a fit range of at least three sizes depending on the brand—the only numbers that matter are the ones that make you look and feel like a perfect 10!

```
411: When hemming
jeans, longer length =
longer legs. Tell your
tailor you'd like to
create a nice "break" in
front and clear the floor
by ¼ inch in back.
```

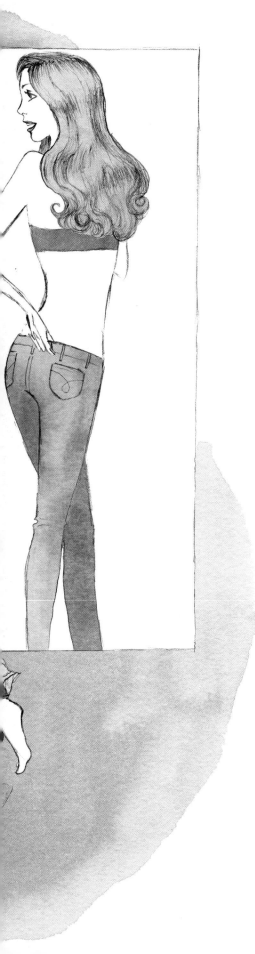

Find Your Fit

More important than the number on the tag is how your potential denim soul mate actually fits. Jeans have their own special rules. For a perfect fit, the waist should sit comfortably just beneath your natural waistline, skim and slim thighs, and gracefully graze your derriere.

> Too tight and too low will constrict and cramp as well as create the always dreaded *muffin top*.
>
> Too tight and too high and *camel toe* can make an appearance.
>
> Too big and too high and you're taking up residence in the suburban-*mom-jean* neighborhood!

To find your perfect rise, keep an eye on your bottom line: you want enough length that the center seam snugly defines your butt. The style of the jeans goes hand in hand with the fit—for more on flattering styles, turn the page.

The Pocket Guide to the
Perfect Pockets

When you're choosing jeans, you'll want to pay close attention to pocket size and placement. A misplaced, misshaped back pocket can devastate the most desirable of jeans. Here are some to avoid.

TOO FAR APART AND/OR TOO LARGE
The equivalent of a neon sign that reads, "Caution: wide load ahead!"

TOO CLOSE TOGETHER AND/OR TOO SMALL
Gives you an undesirable look: unibutt!

TOO HIGH
Will shorten your waist and lengthen your bottom.

TOO LOW
Creates a teardrop effect that is worth crying over.

The ideal pockets are slightly oversized and centered and will make your derriere appear trim and firm and just the right size.

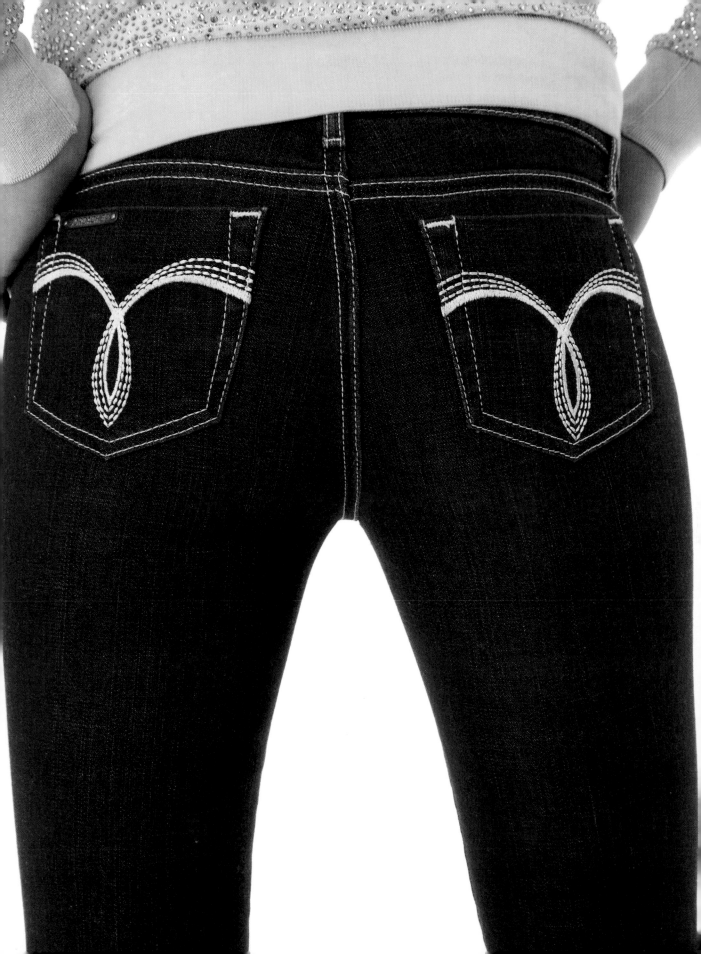

Define your Style

Are you made for *straight, skinny, boot cut, capri,* or *trousers?* The short and long of it, the wide and the narrow of it: jeans for your genes.

411: Avoid overprocessing and embellishment. A jean that is too heavily sandblasted, whiskered, or bejeweled is best left for the sales rack.

STRAIGHT

Slim through the thighs, the straight jean maintains the same width from knee to hem and has an average 8-inch opening. Flattering on most bodies, this chameleon is easily dressed up with heels for an evening out or dressed down with flip-flops for a seaside picnic.

SKINNY

The skinny jean offers a sleek fit that sculpts your legs from waist to ankle and has an average 6-inch opening. Great for small, slight girls, whose petite frames can be overwhelmed by too much fabric, this is a serpentine rock-and-roll staple that is undeniably sexy when the fit is right.

411: A bit of stretch is an important ingredient in skinny jeans. If you go super-skinny, look for a jean with ankle zips to ease the ins and outs.

BOOT CUT

Slim through the thighs, this style is a leg-lengthening favorite that gallops down your thigh, flaring out gently at the knee into a 10-inch opening. Boot-cut jeans are ideal for women with showstopping curves or a less-than-graceful tummy.

411: The ideal flare starts gradually at the knee and increases subtly as it reaches toward the hem. There is nothing worse than a dramatic flare beginning 2 or 3 inches above the hem.

TROUSER

For ladylike sophistica-
tion and style with an
androgynous twist, ease
and elegance, and subtle
sex appeal, the trouser
features a slightly
higher waist, a more
relaxed line, and a
wider opening (12
inches, on average) at
the hem. This jean is
well suited to most
shapes.

411: For a great
trouser silhouette,
try them with a
tucked-in top and a
waist-defining belt.

CAPRI

Wave good-bye to the old-school, constricting high waist and say hello to this made-for-all-seasons achiever. Capris are cut like the straight-leg jean, but hemmed shorter. With an average 8-inch opening, this style is tailor-made for showing off pretty ankles—just make sure the hem caresses the most flattering part of your calf (see the hemline guide on pages 28–29).

411: Try a capri with a slit on the side; this shows a bit more skin and lengthens your leg beautifully!

LIKE A

SIDER

ACT LI

Fitted
to a Tee

In the ladylike closet, the T-shirt most likely appears in the guise of a basic white and fitted one, chic and fabulous with pearls and a favorite cardi. In bohemia, it will shape-shift, sidling up as a slinky deep-V adorned with long lariats.

an *OBVIOUS CHOICE* with a *SUBTLE APPEAL*

Whether you're shopping with Daddy's credit card or what's left of your 401(k), there's a T-shirt out there that's perfect for you.

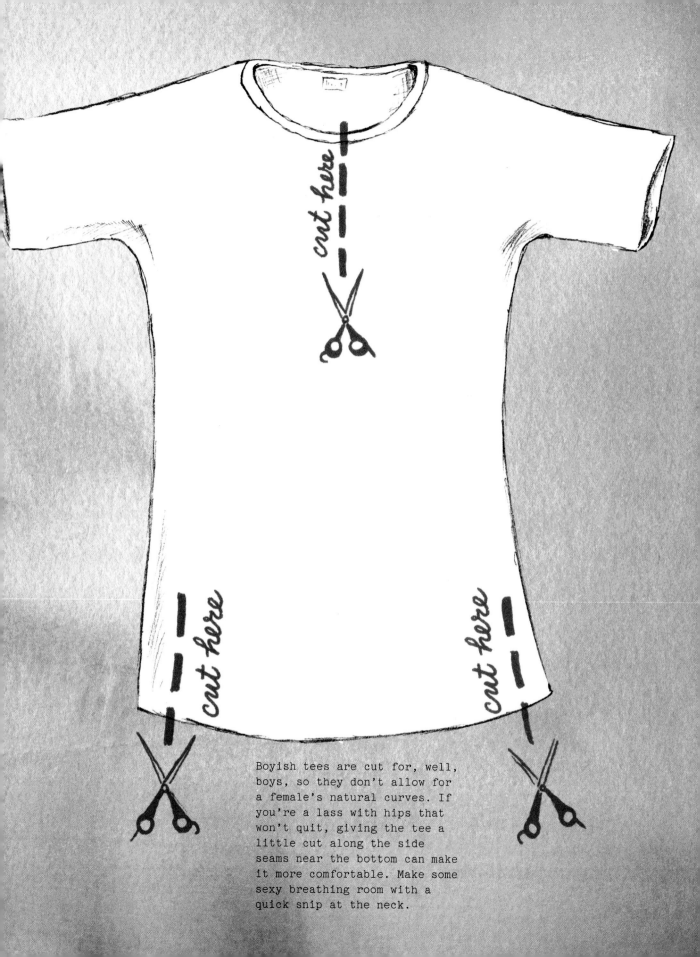

cut here

cut here

cut here

Boyish tees are cut for, well,
boys, so they don't allow for
a female's natural curves. If
you're a lass with hips that
won't quit, giving the tee a
little cut along the side
seams near the bottom can make
it more comfortable. Make some
sexy breathing room with a
quick snip at the neck.

BLUE PERIOD
AMERICAN APPAREL

If you're having a blue
period (or an orange,
red, yellow, or pink
period), choose this
brand for its array of
Rainbow Brite choices.

BARGAIN BUY
FRUIT OF THE LOOM

If you're looking for
"boy tees," think Fruit
of the Loom. They wear
wonderfully on a woman;
are easily dressed up for
a modern twist on a
classic; make a light,
bright beach cover-up;
and come in five-packs
for under $10!

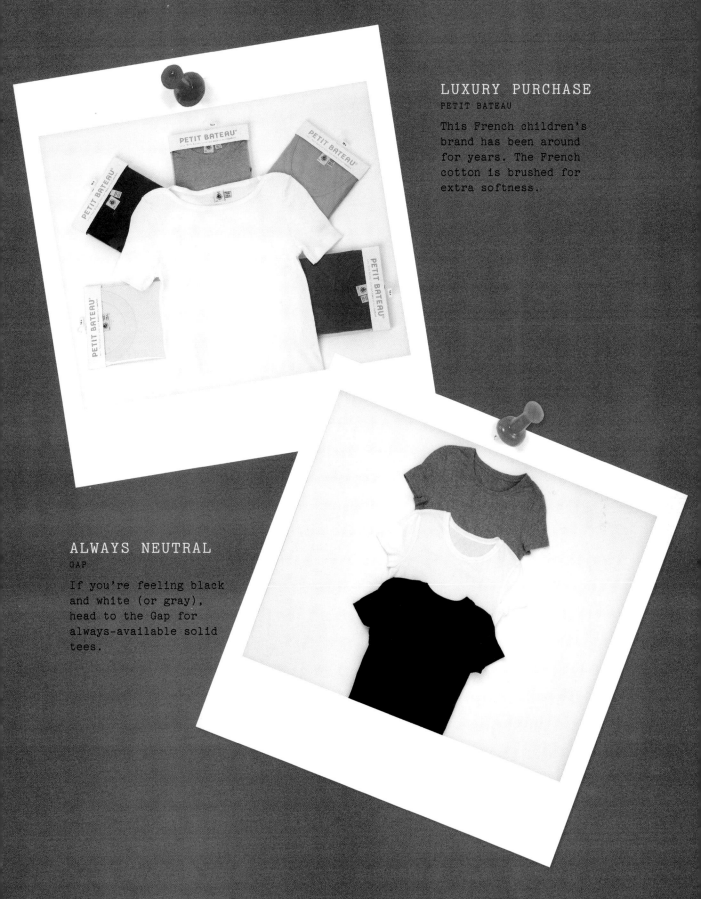

LUXURY PURCHASE
PETIT BATEAU

This French children's brand has been around for years. The French cotton is brushed for extra softness.

ALWAYS NEUTRAL
GAP

If you're feeling black and white (or gray), head to the Gap for always-available solid tees.

Sweaters

Cashmere, Cashmere, *Cashmere*

Cashmere, long a staple of luxe ladies and easy elegance, has become rather affordable. My favorite is a cashmere-alpaca-merino blend that is fluffy and *BE a SOFTY* delicious. Terrific on the slopes, for a cool night at the beach, or layered in lieu of a coat in late fall. If you live in a hot climate, opt for cashmere silk blends. Need I say more?

IRISH ARAN
CABLE FOR REINFORCEMENTS

Wear the history of the
Irish islands on your
sleeve.

COWL NECK
CUDDLE UP

A cowl neck drips and
drapes and still keeps you
cozy.

LACY STITCH SWEATER
SHEERLY THERE

A stitch of lace is subtly
provocative in front of the
fireplace.

V-NECK
V FOR VICTORY

Take the plunge and give your
neck a break.

CREW-NECK CABLE
GO OUT FOR CREW

Row your boat ashore with
caramel-colored cashmere.

Cardigans

NOT just for *GRANDPA!*

This is my favorite style of sweater. Is your *perfect cardi* cute and cropped for that classic fifties look, or big and bohemian? Think argyle for the *all-American*, and embellished for the glam gal. It's adorable over a halter at the office or topping your favorite svelte little dress. Try a cardigan with rhinestone buttons, bracelet sleeves, and a snug fit for a romantic take on an old standby: *mix it up* and try a cardigan on for size!

BOYFRIEND
NOT YOUR BF'S CARDIGAN (ANYMORE)

The "boyfriend" cardi, cut
longer for slouch appeal but
still narrow enough to be
ladylike when belted, has
become a modern classic. Hip,
when it hangs longer than the
hip. Keep it ladylike with
lanky lariats and a sleek fit.

BASIC
ELEMENTARY, MY DEAR

This cardi is anything but basic. A well-cut, single-toned cardi is a TBE . . . Totally awesome, Basically perfect, Essentially elegant.

TUNIC
STRIPES ARE SOLID

Mix it up with mixed and matched patterns. Just keep your tones together and pair with subtle accessories.

RETRO
MARILYN MONROE DID IT

So can you. Be sexy and scandalous with a touch of innocence by pairing barely-there dresses or camis with a fitted, cropped cardi.

EMBELLISHED
GLAM IT UP

Even cover girls catch a chill. Keep the breeze at bay with the sparkle of the sun by contrasting a sheer top with a cardi that glows.

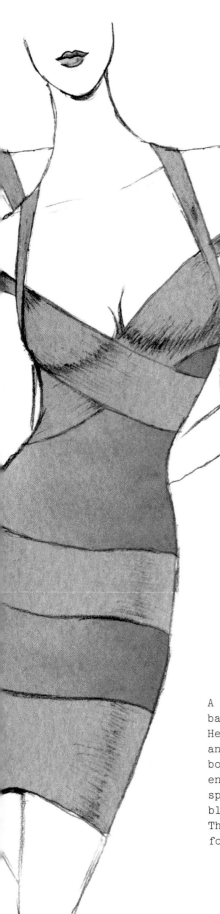

The Perfect Little Dress

and *NO*, it doesn't have to be *BLACK*

Dress it up, dress it down: for office, weekends, dates, and black-tie events, little + black is always an elegant option. But little + vivid = contemporary classic. How do you choose the hue for you? Check our colorful equations in chapter 5.

A modern classic, the bandage dress from Herve Leger is little and perfect. This body-hugging phenomenon runs the color spectrum from bright blue to basic black. There's surely a color for you.

OFFICE

Taking notes or taking
no prisoners: a little
black sheath works at
work just as well for
temps as for CEOs. Think
clean lines, minimal
details, and office-
appropriate hem lengths.

WEEKEND

From the farmers' market to the dog run, sweet, soft details make a black dress sunny enough for Sundays. Look for flowing fabrics, empire waistlines, and a touch of whimsy.

DATE

First date, first kiss,
first anniversary: sexy
and slinky but not too
revealing. Get him to
ask the right questions
by balancing a plunging
neckline with a demure
hem length (or vice
versa).

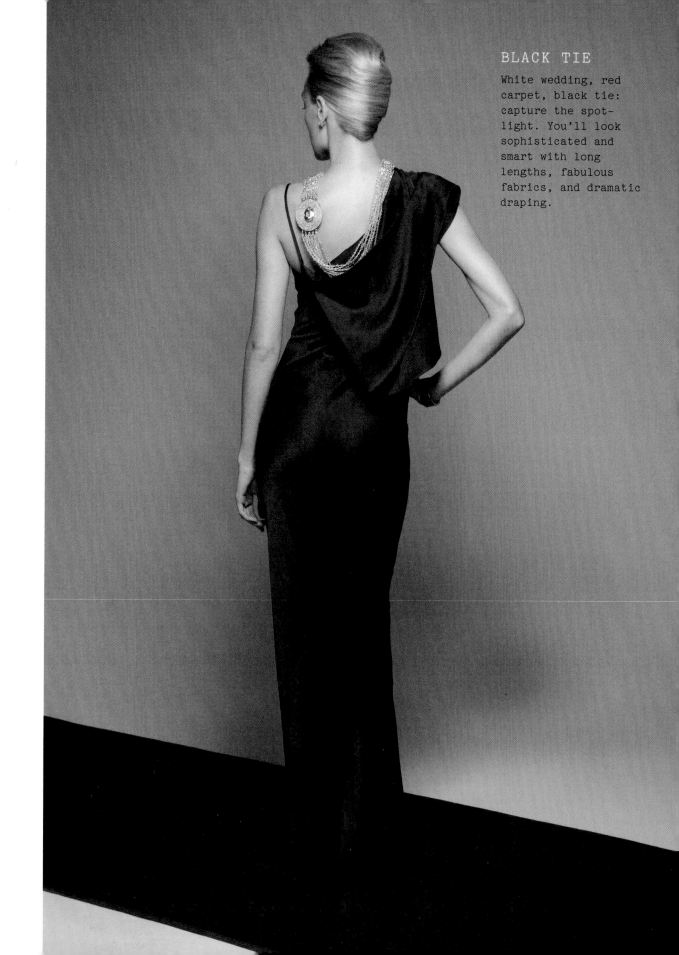

BLACK TIE

White wedding, red carpet, black tie: capture the spotlight. You'll look sophisticated and smart with long lengths, fabulous fabrics, and dramatic draping.

OFFICE

Leading a meeting
or hoping for
a permanent
position? You've
got their atten-
tion. Seek out
rich colors,
soft lines,
and a demure
décolletage.

WEEKEND

Liven up the
brunch brigade.
Vivid tones, bold
patterns, and
casual fabrics
render you
fabulous for
sipping Bellinis
and swapping
ladies'-locker-
room stories.

DATE

Who cares who
asked whom? Royal
gem tones show
him that you're a
princess; a
sweeping neckline
shows him who
rules the roost.

BLACK TIE

All that glitters
is golden:
shimmer in the
moonlight with
luminescent
gowns. Your
hemline should
sweep the floor;
your head should
be in the stars.

a great Suit
brings greatness

You need only one or two suits to mix and match with your sweaters, chemises, scarves, and shoes. If purchased properly, they will last for years and give you endless styling opportunities.

Here are some suits to consider:

If *flirty and feminine* is your calling card, choose a *skirt suit.* It's best in neutral tweeds, with a form-fitting jacket and an A-line or pleated skirt.

If you gravitate toward *men's suiting,* go glen plaid or consider a *sexy black tuxedo cut.*

Be mindful of fabric: tropical wool with a little stretch is the way to go. (Check the label to make sure the suit is made mostly of wool and not of some synthetic.)

a *WELL-FITTED SUIT* exudes confidence, *POWER,* and *POLISH*

if you dream of *EFFORTLESS CHIC,* make like Savile Row even if you live in Sioux Falls or Schenectady, and slip into *A PERFECTLY TAILORED SUIT*

Fashion Transformers

Leave the basics behind and go from *day to night* and *office to weekend.*

Office to Evening

Powerhouse from nine to five, lady of leisure from five to nine: with an **early** breakfast meeting, a power lunch, and an afternoon of conferences, there's no time to change before your dinner date. Fear not. When you get to the bar, slip your evening clutch out of your tote, and check your jacket with the rest of your belongings. Add a bit of lip gloss and eyeliner, and order a martini while you wait.

Make your career ensembles do overtime: *from Monday to Friday* you work. Weekends, you work it. When you're at the office, wear a matched suit with a dressy chemise and ladylike heels. When you're heading out on Sunday, pair your boardroom blazer with an essential tee, flats, and your comfiest jeans for a brunch-time bonanza.

Chemise

A suit is nothing without a beautiful shirt; I use "chemise" here to mean a classic blouse with buttons. It will look:

classic under a suit

neat under a cardi

casually sexy under a cashmere sweater with a bit of lace peeking out

Whether bowed, ruched, or simply an oxford in men's shirting, consider the chemise the white T-shirt of your dress-up essentials. I suspect that once you have one, you'll quickly find that you need two or three. Or four.

BUTTON UP *for* IMPECCABLE *style*

Accessories
the *icing* on the *cake*

GO TO CAPRI WITHOUT
LEAVING THE BLOCK

Turquoise skies and
coral sunsets can be
yours every weekend with
effervescent baubles and
bags; a silk cerulean
scarf will keep your
hair neat on the way to
the beach even when the
convertible is just a
rental.

OFFICE
POWER THROUGH YOUR POINTS

At the office, conservative colors get a punch from bold swings of bright bijou tones. Oversized beads, bangles, and totes add knockout flair to everyday wear.

Whether you're heading to the office or out and about, getting red-carpet ready or primping for Prince Charming, frost yourself appropriately.

BLACK TIE
GO HEAVY METAL

Never be afraid to wear
your sunglasses at
night. Add some razzle-
dazzle with boots that
are made for dancing,
rock-star rocks, and a
clutch that keeps on
shining while the cute
coat-check guy keeps an
eye on your metallic
tote.

DATE
UNLEASH YOUR INNER ANIMAL

The laws of the jungle apply when you're looking for a mate. Survive as the fittest in slinky serpentine chains, animal prints, and lipstick-red patent pumps.

Your Signature Piece

NEVER leave home WITHOUT IT

To become an icon, or at least to feel like one, you will need a signature piece. In brief, it is your *"Carrie" necklace,* your *"Blair" headband,* or your *"Ellen" sneakers.* You will wear it with pride, cherish it, and own it.

My signature color is blue. Whether it's a sweater, a jacket, or even my jeans, I wear blue nearly every day. I also have my signature necklaces, which haven't left my neck in years: a deer head and an onyx-wolf pendant that represent my backwoods-Michigan roots; a golden horseshoe with a single diamond gifted to me that keeps me feeling lucky; and a diamond cross that my grandmother left me.

ODDS ARE your signature piece won't be something that you go and find so much as *SOMETHING THAT HAS FOUND YOU*

Investment Purchases
coat, sunglasses, bag

Just because these pieces cost more doesn't mean they aren't basics. Some essentials are expensive but are worth every penny. Unlike stock options, they will not decrease in value and are a most worthy investment in your fashion portfolio.

COAT
BASIC TRENCH COAT
My top basic coat pick is a khaki Burberry trench. A trench is timeless, perfect for seasonal transitions, and it easily morphs from one incarnation to the next. Toss it on with yellow Wellies; wear it unbuttoned and belted in back; personalize it with a colorful cashmere scarf.

411: Buy a liner for winter.

STATEMENT COAT
FOR WINTER
Cold climes require a bold winter anorak. Look for a coat that will keep you warm but also set you apart. In the winter, your coat is the face you show the world on a daily basis.

SUNGLASSES
Start with one amazing pair of expensive sunglasses to take your style up a notch. Then drop into your local accessories shop for a baker's dozen of cheapie pairs in every color of this season's rainbow.

BAG
The goal here is to find one high-quality bag that may set you back some cash—even upwards of $200—but will last forever, and then you can expand your bag horizons with less costly choices.

411: Don't spend more than $50 on a designer knockoff.

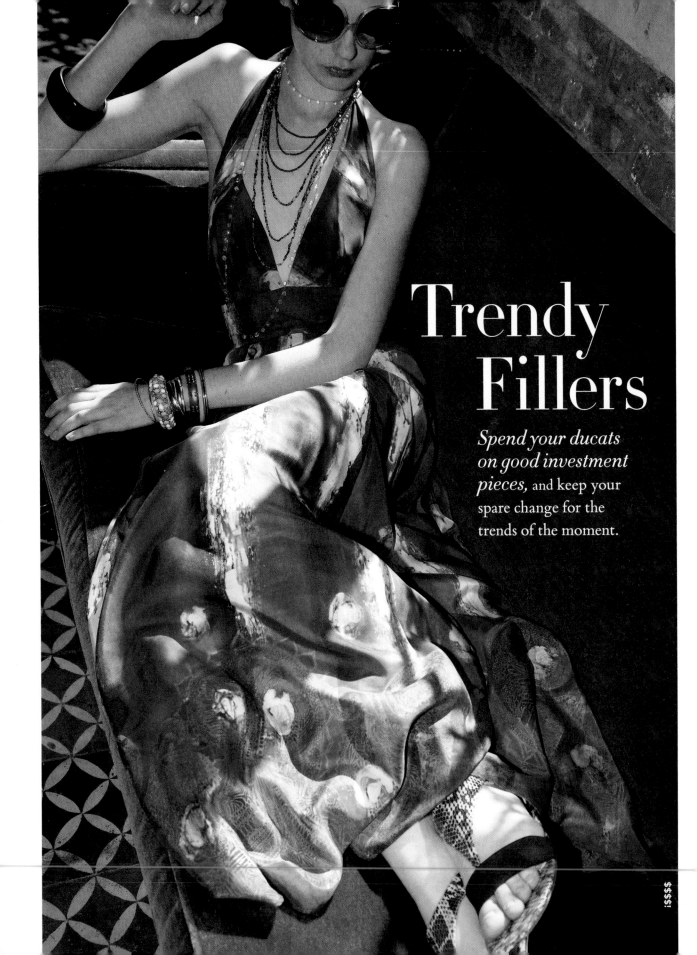

Trendy Fillers

Spend your ducats on good investment pieces, and keep your spare change for the trends of the moment.

The stuff that's on the runway in platinum is often recast in sterling and readily available at stores nationwide. Top-model looks for bargain-basement prices: I call that a win-win. Who's who? Guess which lounging lady overpaid? Answer at bottom.

BARGAIN BUY!

Who's Who?

Uptown meets downtown.
Guess who shops on the
Upper East Side and who
shops on the Lower East
Side? Answer at bottom.

3.
CLOSET
CASE

Now you know what you absolutely need. Before you decide what you absolutely *want,* we're going to tackle the Dark Hole that is your closet.

Each season, I purge my costume closet, and I suggest that you do the same with yours. The three magic words for the closet case?

EDIT!
EDIT!
EDIT!

Get rid of those skeletons of seasons past and make room for your fashionable future.

Lingerie

Accessories

Stockings

Laundry

Exorcise
Your Closet

Don't let your head spin around—clean out your demons so your closet can be your sanctuary.

Easy stuff first ...

1 TOTALLY BASIC ESSENTIALS

Set your TBE's aside.

2 ABSOLUTE TO-DIE-FOR FAVORITES

You love them, you love them, you love them.

3 NEEDS SOME LOVING

Would-be go-to goodies except for runaway buttons, torn linings, stains . . .

Now the hard part ...

4 THE REJECTS

This might hurt, but you'll thank me later. Be merciless! Here's what goes into this pile:

ANYTHING YOU HAVEN'T WORN in over a year.

THE CLONES. If you love black pencil skirts, my guess is that you have way too many of them. Choose the top three; ditch the rest.

LUXURY ITEMS YOU'RE KEEPING JUST BECAUSE THEY WERE EXPENSIVE. If you've never worn it, you never will. Consider doing consignment retail.

LAST YEAR'S TRENDIEST. If you can't bring yourself to sport it, get rid of it!

"I LOVE IT BUT IT LOOKS AWFUL ON ME." Also known as the Jeans of Torture or the Dress from Ten Pounds Ago.

a *WELL-EDITED* and *GLORIOUSLY GROOMED CLOSET* is a glamour girl's best style secret!

yes

maybe

CHIC TECHNIQUE

AS YOU GO THROUGH YOUR CLOSET AND DRAWERS, if you find something you haven't worn as recently as a few weeks ago, try it on in front of a full-length mirror.

SEE HOW YOU LOOK standing, sitting, and making basic daily gestures like hailing a cab or flirting.

DON'T FORGET THE 360-DEGREE MIRROR INSPECTION: Take careful notice of the "danger zones": bustline, under-arms, buttons and zippers, shoulders, pelvic region, hips, and tummy.

ENJOY BEING THE STAR OF YOUR OWN MONTAGE: This is your chick-flick makeover, your *Pretty Woman* or *Clueless* or *She's All That* moment. Play your own personal soundtrack in the background.

BELIEVE IN THE POWER OF THE PURGE! Whatever you do, do not give up halfway through this terrifying task! I promise you, the end result will be worth every bead of sweat you put into it.

Say Good-bye....

Now that you have all of your clothing in four style piles, it's time to hang, fold, purge, and restore.

COMBINE 1 & 2 Hang your TBE's and your to-die-for favorites in your now cavernous closet, first by type—shirts, skirts, pants, suits, and dresses—and then by color. Now your closet is as fun to look at as it is to use!

ALTER 3 Give your tired, worn clothing the love it needs by calling in a master—the tailor. In the next section, you'll replace your best friend with someone who is handy with a sewing machine and will breathe new life into your old garments.

EDIT 4 Say farewell and complete your ritual exorcism. Put all your rejects into a garbage bag to be gifted, sold, or donated to a local charity.

411: Shops like the Container Store sell plastic boxes and shelving options that can help you turn your closet into a place of invigoration instead of despair.

BE BOLD. BE TOUGH.
Remember, you've got to
BE CRUEL TO BE KIND!

Make Your Tailor Your BFF

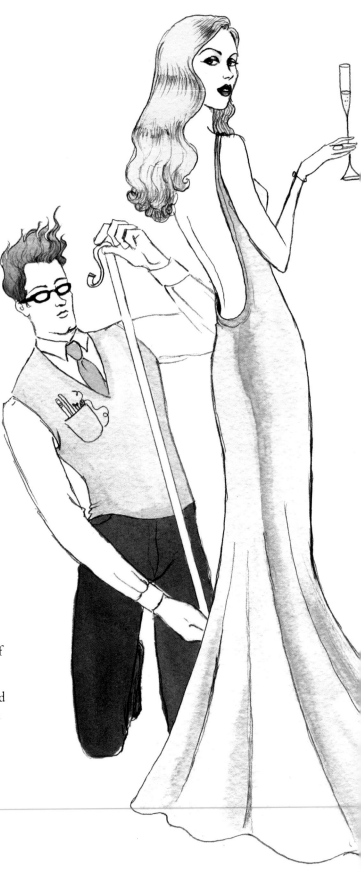

Every item of clothing you see gracing the glorious screen or the magazines has been tailored and customized to fit. "Ready to wear" more often means "ready to be picked up at the tailor's." Having a tailor alter your garments can make a world of difference, and it isn't necessarily very expensive.

To find yours:

ASK FRIENDS AND FAMILY to recommend a skilled local alterations mistress, or check the yellow pages or bulletin boards at local shops.

INQUIRE AT YOUR LOCAL FABRIC STORE or dry cleaner; they almost always know the best talent in town. Many dry cleaners also have someone on staff who does alterations.

IF YOU LIVE IN A MORE URBAN SETTING, high-end boutiques usually have in-house tailors that you can outsource.

411: Ask an unfamiliar tailor to do a small job, like hemming a pair of pants, before you ask him to alter your wedding dress.

411: Take your favorite dress, shirt, or suit to your trusted tailor and have her take it apart and then put it back together. Then she will always have a pattern to use whenever you find an inspiring fabric. Talk about customized individual personal style!

411: Revamp a boring coat by having your tailor line it with a crazy color or pattern you don't have the guts to wear on the outside.

TAILOR TO-DO LIST

THE FREAK-OUT: My pants are too long.
THE FIX: Bring the shoes you'll wear with them to the tailor and try them on together to make sure you get the right hem length.

THE FREAK-OUT: My waistband is too tight.
THE FIX: There will usually be enough fabric in the seams of pants and skirts to allow releasing up to an inch.

THE FREAK-OUT: I lost weight and now none of my clothes fit!
THE FIX: Dresses and skirts can often be taken in. And a tailor can easily debulk a coat and slim it down.

THE FREAK-OUT: This cardigan is so *boring*!
THE FIX: Dazzle up a dull basic by giving buttons a sparkly upgrade.

THE FREAK-OUT: This skirt makes my legs look fat.
THE FIX: Check our handy hemline guide (pages 28–29) and then have your tailor trim to add a mile to your gams.

THE FREAK-OUT: The zipper on my jeans is broken.
THE FIX: Your tailor can replace it!

Make Your
Cobbler
Your
Second BFF

Just because you don't have tiny elves to take care of your shoes doesn't mean you're destined to click-clack around in heels worn down to the nub. Your shoemaker can help you maintain your shoes so they can keep going as long as you can. Especially if you live in an urban area, where miles of pavement can turn the nicest leather soles to mush in mere days, remember that the shoemaker is not just for repairs, but for pretreatments that will keep new shoes healthy for years to come.

SHOE R$_X$

LOW-COST, LIFE-PROLONGING OPERATIONS

RUBBER DEMI-SOLES
FUNCTION: Protect soles and help prevent slips
FOR: All shoes

HEEL PROTECTORS
FUNCTION: Give a necessary extra barrier between high heels and the ground
FOR: Sexy stilettos and precious pumps

WEATHERPROOFING SPRAYS AND OILS
FUNCTION: Will keep shoes happy whether there's rain, snow, or sunshine
FOR: Soft suede and leather

REGULAR POLISHING
FUNCTION: Keeps leather from cracking; adds to a more refined look overall
FOR: Leather shoes and boots

411: Your shoes' ultimate nemesis is salt on a snowy sidewalk. Salt will eat through most protectants and quickly damage surfaces. If you are stuck in salt, wipe your shoes with a damp paper towel or a Wet One as soon as possible.

DIY ACTIONS FOR TAKING CARE OF YOUR SHOES (AND YOUR FEET)

SUEDE HEEL GRIPS
FUNCTION: Give a nice cushion and grip efficiently; softer than foam or corduroy products
FOR: Shoes that leave your foot skidding forward

MOLESKIN
FUNCTION: Protects against blisters in sensitive spots
FOR: Everyone, especially in summer

BAND-AIDS
FUNCTION: Come in handy if moleskin lets you down
FOR: Tender toes and heels

ATHLETIC GELLED INSOLES
FUNCTION: Lend a bit of comfort
FOR: Everyone, not just athletes

GELLED MINI-PADS
FUNCTION: Placed in shoes under the balls of your feet, turn negative space positive and put the spring back in your step
FOR: Open-toed shoes that are a bit big in front or back

Merostar Lily
$8.00
Bunch

INSPIR

4.
THINK
LIKE A STYLIST

Style is timeless.

While trends come and go, an understanding of style is forever. Once you learn to think like a stylist, you'll develop the ability to translate exterior inspirations into your own personal palette, creating elegant and eye-pleasing combinations of garments that suit and flatter the figure. Coco Chanel said, "Fashion is not something that exists in dresses only. Fashion is in the sky, in the street, fashion has to do with ideas, the way we live, what is happening." Thinking like a stylist requires that you look within and without—inside yourself to understand who you are and what you want to express, and outside yourself to take cues from the vibrant planet you live on.

The lesson here:

INSPIRATION COMES FROM EVERYWHERE

Thinking like a stylist doesn't start when you open the closet door—it begins the moment you open your eyes in the morning.

How many times have you heard someone say (or maybe found yourself saying):

"If only I could look like _____."

"Why can't I dress like _____?"

"I'll never be as fashionable as _____."

We're all subject to the inevitable comparisons, the "I wishes." Well, let's all stop wishing and do something about it. Instead of worrying about what others think of the way we look, let's pay closer attention to how we feel and what we think. Let's consider how style can be a reflection of our individuality instead of whether or not we look like the latest It Girl.

you don't need to
BE ANYONE
but you

block out
red-carpet unreality
and *BECOME YOUR
OWN STYLIST*

Style Armada

DON'T WANT IT,
don't need it,
don't have to have it

Here's the insider's perspective: it's important to remember that every image of a celebrity you see is the result of teamwork. Most of us, being mortal, don't have a style armada to mold and pamper us into picture-perfect shape every day. So we need to rely on ourselves, and make the best of what we've got by harnessing the insider secrets that work and ignoring those that don't.

Past Perfect

When creating characters and trying to make them look as authentic as possible through their style, I examine their history. Where they come from, and what decisions, choices, and experiences have led them to their current persona are fundamental in defining their fashions. For example, one very wealthy teen TV character I was designing had gone to summer camp in Switzerland and boarding school in France. As she explores the world and absorbs and recognizes the elements that are beautiful to her, her style is enhanced and becomes a reflection of who she is. I gave her a worldly air by having her sport vintage scarves from Parisian flea markets and custom boots from Milan paired with perfectly distressed Levi's, creating the aura of this all-American thoroughbred with European savoir faire in one single outfit. Her ensembles feel natural, authentic, and original because they combine where she came from with where she has traveled.

While dwelling on the past is never a good thing, by taking a step back and looking at your experiences through a lens of acceptance and not regret, you can mine them for inspiration and insight. This is a key element of thinking like a stylist. You can use my stylist secrets to uncover the shiniest facets of your own history, and by extension, a facet of your ideal look. Instead of compiling your list of perfect must-haves solely from the mannequins in shop windows, I want you to look backward in order to look forward, to see what experiences you have had that make you unique and then incorporate them into your personal style. Your clogs from Holland will go great with that leather jacket from the flea market in Florence you bought while backpacking through Europe. The handbag you inherited from Grandma will look thoroughly modern with your favorite blue jeans. Speaking of which, don't let color get you down.

WHO YOU WERE is essential to *WHO YOU ARE*

5.
COLOR
ME BEAUTIFUL

Artists use the world around them as inspiration for their creations. So do stylists, and so can you. The cerulean blue of the sky becomes a layered chiffon tunic; the vivid hues of a fiery sunset translate into a dress so hot it practically burns your skin. Creating art involves seeing things for what they could be, not just for what they are.

In this chapter, you'll learn how to identify your most complementary colors and use them to your advantage. The best part is that you can be anything you want to be. A doctor, a judge, the president. A sun-streaked summer in August, a fiery autumn in October, and an ice princess in January. Think of yourself as the canvas and paint with your clothes, covering yourself in beautifully arranged colors that frame your face.

Defining an actor's color palette is one of the first concrete styling steps I take when I design a character. Same goes for you!

How to tell which spectrum of the rainbow has your pot of gold? In the pages that follow, you'll identify which season's characteristics sound most like you.

NO FLOWER IS A SINGLE COLOR

SPRI

THE CHEEKY BLUSH OF A PEONY

This is the season to consider lipstick and shoes that could have been grown in a garden, a silk scarf like a glass of lemonade, a romantic top dotted with flowers. Spring is a promise, a picnic, a walk in the country. This is the season when colors are soft and sleepy from being hidden away all winter.

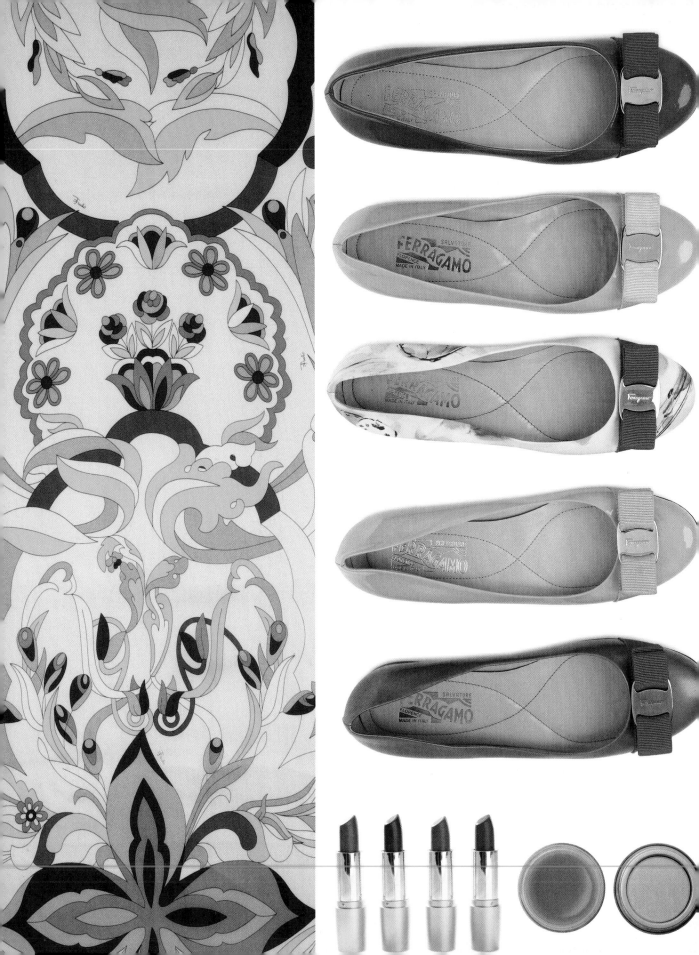

The Fair Maiden

Do you blush easily? Do summer photos show you with a smattering of freckles across your cheeks?

SPRING

HAIR: blond, strawberry blond, copper, or golden brown

EYES: blue or green

SKIN: creamy and fair with a rosy, pink undertone

YOUR BEST COLORS: blush and bashful, citrine green, perfectly peach, robin's egg blue

YOUR PRECIOUS METAL: powdery rose gold

SUM

BLONDES HAVE MORE FUN

Summer is the radio on too loud, a big
pair of sunglasses, the sweet smell of
coconut. Warm and neutral, golden
and earthy, shimmering and vibrant,
drenched in sunshine and light. Satu-
rated tones recall a morning at the
beach with the sun in your eyes, an
afternoon driving down roads edged
by palm trees with the top down on
the convertible, a row of Art Deco
buildings redone with a modern slant.

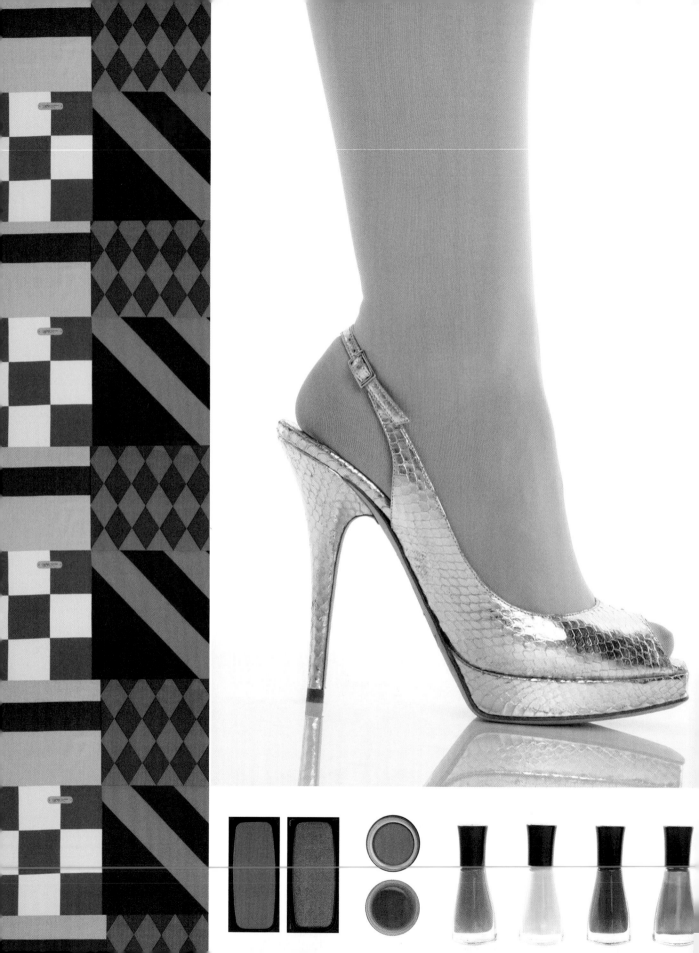

The Golden Goddess

Are you quick to tan? Does your hair lighten naturally in the sun?

Summer

HAIR: platinum blond, golden blond, or ash brown
EYES: blue or green
SKIN: translucent beige with golden undertones
YOUR BEST COLORS: raging red, grass green, canary yellow, torrid turquoise
YOUR PRECIOUS METAL: sun-drenched 24K gold

UMN

FALL INTO FIRE

Autumn is when summer sizzles into the cool dark of winter, with a frenzy of furious color along the way. Pumpkins and winter squashes and rows of red-cheeked apple trees, ambers and jewel tones. Autumn is resplendent with rich, passionate colors that lead us from summer's brights to winter's cool ice.

The Woodland Nymph

Are you a fiery redhead? Are your green eyes often confused with hazel?

Autumn

HAIR: auburn, dark honey, or dirty blond
EYES: amber, hazel, or steel
SKIN: pale peach, golden brown, olive
YOUR BEST COLORS: beautiful Bordeaux, hunter green, autumn amber, midnight blue
YOUR PRECIOUS METAL: fiery bronze

Winter glistens with embers and diamonds. The icicles dangle from the dark, lacy trees. But this season is also warm and inviting, like a lush rug in front of a fireplace or a cashmere sweater so cozy you never want to put on anything else. Think Snow White, with dark eyes, red lips, and a beautiful gown in deep burgundy and icy lilac.

TER

FROSTED WITH GLAMOUR

The Ice Princess

Are you an African queen? Do you look like Snow White?

Winter

HAIR: ebony, dark brown, or white blond
EYES: blue-gray, black-brown, or gray-green
SKIN: lustrous ebony with blue undertones or pale ivory with a delicate pink tone
YOUR BEST COLORS: magically magenta, jade with jealousy, sterling silver, royal amethyst
YOUR PRECIOUS METAL: icy platinum

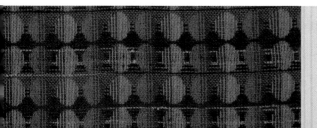
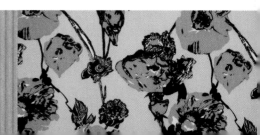

Frame your visage
with an appropriate
color corsage!

Frame *Your* Face

choosing your *IDEAL* palette

Use *your best colors to frame your face.* You want accessories that relate to the tone of your skin and your hair. When styling your canvas, put the colors that give you the glow up top and leave the others down below. This doesn't mean that you can't *integrate your favorite colors into your outfits.* If red is all the rage but not on your best-color page, use it as an accent: think red shoes, a red belt, or a red skirt. This might even become your signature hue. If the color of taxicabs inspires you but leaves you looking pale and washed out, pick up a vibrant yellow bag. Just don't wear the color near your face!

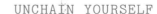

UNCHAIN YOURSELF

Looking through rose-colored glasses is great, but make sure you choose a colored frame for your shades that showcases your face.

Frame-Your-Face •
Accessories

GILDED AGE

The Midas touch can get
you in trouble; make sure
necklaces and earrings
give you a glow and don't
turn you to stone.

don't be a
MAD HATTER—
because
*HEADWEAR
MATTERS!*

6.
WHO ARE YOU TODAY?

In this chapter, you'll meet five fashion archetypes based on Hollywood glamour, vintage fashion, and stunning contemporary pieces. Each of these muses makes a wonderful catalyst for inspiration. If you wish, create a different character every day. Your style should be fluid.

WHO WILL YOU BE TOMORROW?

Be Inspired

CLASSIC   ECLECTIC   NATURAL

A-muse *yourself*

DRAMATIC

ROMANTIC

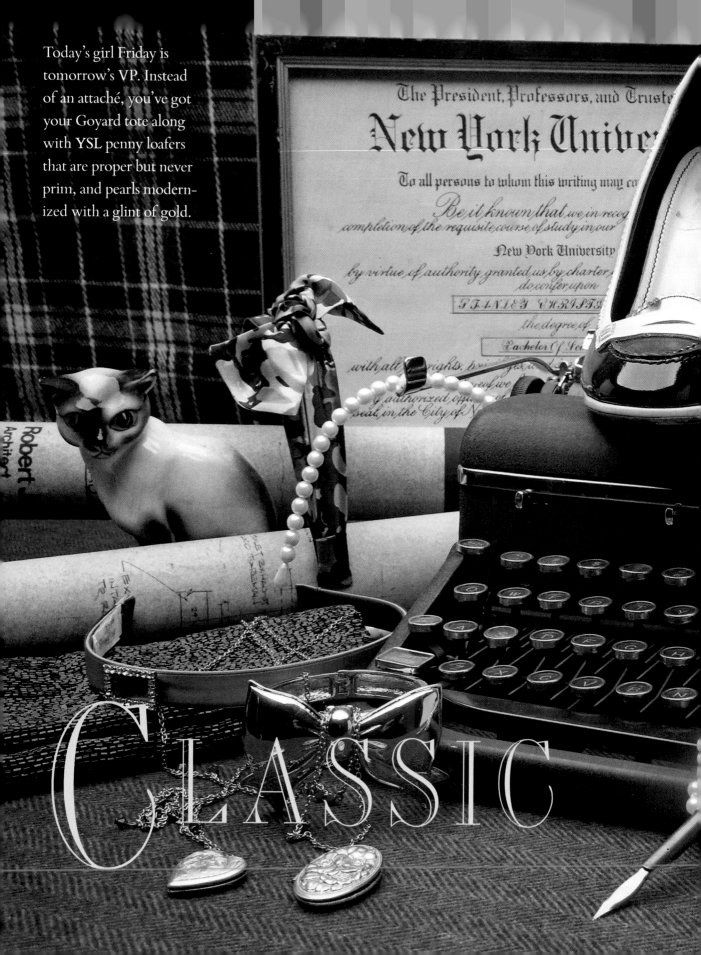

Today's girl Friday is tomorrow's VP. Instead of an attaché, you've got your Goyard tote along with YSL penny loafers that are proper but never prim, and pearls modernized with a glint of gold.

CLASSIC

MY GIRL FRIDAY

Ladylike, with Just a Touch of Mystery . . .

Controlled. Conservative. Smart.
A classic never makes a spectacle
of herself—but she also never
gets lost in the shadows. Her
silhouettes are tailored and crisp,
politely mixed with hints of soft
and subtle. Imagine a made-
to-measure herringbone blazer
with a blouse in delicate dupioni,
or crisp men's shirting under a
supple sweater. Petite, discreet
accessories adorn her: a charming
charm bracelet, perfect pearls, and
of course a headband *assorti*. The
classic is thinking about the first
day on the job, and she's already
got her eye on the corner office.

Eclectic

CURIOUS AND CLEVER

Breakfast in Bali, cocktails on Melrose . . . Let your boho bag brim with carved wooden beads from Africa, a delicately embroidered clutch swiped from your grandmother's bureau, and slinky scarves of silk.

Electric. Always extraordinary, never ordinary. Wild and wonderful. The eclectic favors slouchy boots, slinky tanks, sun-kissed skin, and perfect beach-bum hair. An apparent highbred from bohemia (but is she really?), she knows to mix high and low, and does so through elaborate layering choices. Think a boyfriend cardigan draped over a slinky tank and denim shorts, complete with long necklaces and armfuls of bangles. The cardigan is her sister's, the tank was picked up at a Barneys free-for-all, the carved wooden bracelets are from her last trip to Bali, and the necklaces were a gift from an old gypsy on the boardwalk at Venice Beach. The eclectic is a free spirit just as likely to be listening to the Grateful Dead as planning her next escapade in Southeast Asia.

Unconventional and Unforgettable

NATURAL

Fresh from your sailing
race in Amagansett . . . Go
from fore to aft with a
weathered leather satchel,
a patterned kerchief, and
stones of cerulean blue.

SMART AND SIMPLE

Casual Ease and Elegance

All-natural, all-American—by way of
European tomboy chic. The natural
goes from safari to seaplane without
missing a beat. An energetic demeanor
and an informal manner set the tone
for her style, and a mix-and-match
wardrobe of unconstructed silhouettes
lets her breeze through any situation.
Note the smattering of masculinity
via a great men's watch or a crisp
boyish dress shirt that lends her style
a charmingly androgynous panache.
The natural goes on picnics with
perfectly chilled bottles of rosé and
cucumber sandwiches with the crusts
still on. She can ride like a dream and
has even been known to enjoy a fox
hunt. And it is the rare fellow who is
not charmed as much by the way she
looks in his shirt as by her insouciant,
casual air.

DRAMATIC

Bring chic out of the shadows. Line your dressing room with crocodile boots with the highest of heels, crystal-ized clutches, and brilliant baubles that always catch the spotlight.

FILM NOIR *VEDETTE*

A Vixen with Glamorous Tendencies

Bordello chic. Vampy, not trampy.
Little Ms. Dramatic dreams of
cascading gowns of gold, stones that
sparkle, sophisticated textiles, lacy
stockings, and a little too much kohl
around the eyes. She likes extreme
fashion, and is happy to don the most
severe lines or the softest of
silhouettes. She knows how to work a
room and be the center of attention,
but she will never overdo it and fall
victim to stereotypes. Over-the-top
top? She pairs it with a chic,
understated accessory. The simplest of
garments? She compensates for
straight lines with the most elaborate
bijous. Her treasure chest is filled to
capacity with statement necklaces,
cocktail rings, and discreet pieces to
wear in between. And her little black
book? Just as overflowing . . .

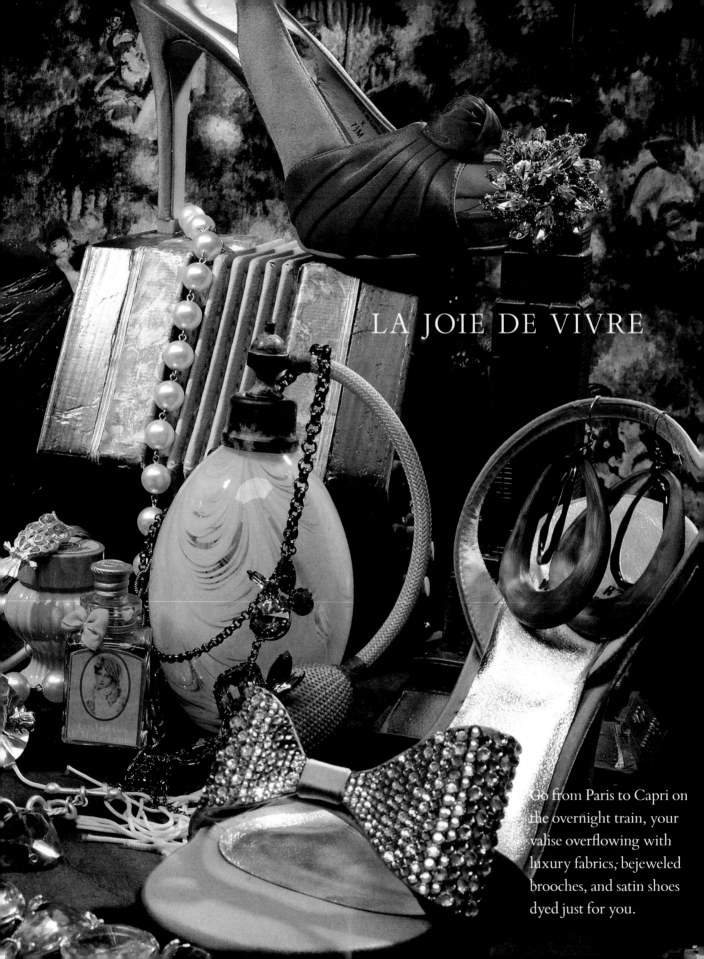

LA JOIE DE VIVRE

Go from Paris to Capri on the overnight train, your valise overflowing with luxury fabrics, bejeweled brooches, and satin shoes dyed just for you.

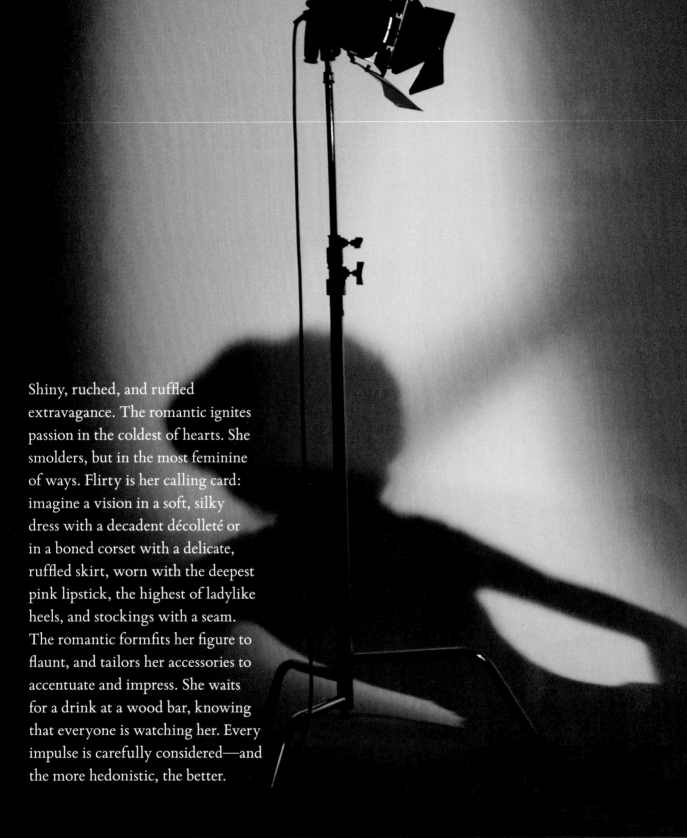

Shiny, ruched, and ruffled extravagance. The romantic ignites passion in the coldest of hearts. She smolders, but in the most feminine of ways. Flirty is her calling card: imagine a vision in a soft, silky dress with a decadent décolleté or in a boned corset with a delicate, ruffled skirt, worn with the deepest pink lipstick, the highest of ladylike heels, and stockings with a seam. The romantic formfits her figure to flaunt, and tailors her accessories to accentuate and impress. She waits for a drink at a wood bar, knowing that everyone is watching her. Every impulse is carefully considered—and the more hedonistic, the better.

A Graceful Creature of Luxury

STYLE

7.
ELEMENTS OF
STYLE

Shampoo, condition, rinse, repeat.

Style is much like hair care. The right combination of products can give you a fab do—however, celeb hairdressers worldwide agree it is important to regularly vary their use to keep tendrils fresh and fancy! The same goes for *la mode*. Create fun and fearless fashions by trying out new things. Be your own paper doll and wash those style split ends right out of your hair!

try a *GLAMOROUS UPDO*
for day, and something
SOFT AND SENSUAL
for night

Erica Baum, *Shampoo*, 2008

Style Sudoku

Layering the basics is a key way to personalize your style. So play style sudoku and add up these mix-and-match pieces for a *fresh take on fashion.*

Skirts
A-lines
and Pencils and Minis,
Oh My!

Skirts are flirty and feminine. A woman in a skirt has power that a woman in a pants suit can only dream of. Think feline grace and womanly wiles, or just plain adorable.

FLIP AND FLATTER

A pleated mini will make
them murmur. Keep them
guessing with a pair of
opaque tights.

CHEER THIS!

Rah! Rah! is everyday appropriate in gradated charmeuse.

LOOK AT ME

Sandra Dee plaids are warm and cozy. Pair a heavy skirt with a slim-fitting top so your figure won't be overwhelmed. Fishnets and boots add a touch of sass to this picture of class.

401(K) PORTFOLIO

A feminine top with a solid
feminine skirt—it's a wrap!

HOT TIN ROOF

This pencil skirt heats up
with a vertically lined
blouse. Highlight your waist
with this skinny black belt
and lengthen your legs with
perfect black pumps.

Luxury Toppings

We've already covered your Totally Basic Essentials, which are the foundation of your everyday dressing. Now it's time to add to them. These architectural trimmings take your black pants and your skinny jeans from totally basic to totally fabulous.

Take the sloop out for a spin on Sunday; on Monday, pair this striped sailor top with a sunny boyfriend cardi anchored with a tiered red rope necklace.

411: Feeling extra *Pirates of Penzance*? Add a silk kerchief pillaged from a second-hand treasure trove.

MARTHA'S VINEYARD

Sail away in an oxford-blue chemise. Swimmingly slimming horizontal stripes on a lace-stitched sweater vest will keep them coming up for air.

ADMIRAL VS. FIRST MATE

Just because there's a whole palette of color out there doesn't mean you always have to be Crayola bright. Layering tonal hues can be a treat any day of the week.

EMBELLISH YOUR RATTAN

This silk cami is a summer stand-alone. The pattern makes it extra interesting, the cardigan carries it over into autumn.

ROCKER-CHIC BATIK

This cashmere V-neck is a chic batik. Color is good, but the Technicolor dream coat is best left to Broadway, so this bright top gets a toned-down jacket.

Pants

a *Must-Have*
Even if You Are
Pantophobic!

Now that you know which pants fit you like a charm, it's time to add a dash of panache with fabulous fabrics and daring details—and, of course, the stylish pieces you pair them with.

STORM THE BASTILLE!

Patriotism isn't just for the Fourth of July. Sport it all summer long with crisp white wide-leg trousers.

411: Make sure white pants are lined, or have the pockets removed.

SHEERS AND STRIPES

What's good enough for Grandpa
is even better for you when
lines are tailored, heels are
high, and blouses are sheer
enough to see through.

TONAL TWEEDS

A contemporary twist on a
classic. A touch of shimmer
takes tweed from matronly to
of-the-moment. With a matte
jacket, you will shine, but
not like a disco ball.

GO GREEN!

Make this Audrey classic contemporary by sporting it in bold colors. Balance candy colors with neutral tops and accessories.

TANGERINE DREAM

Show off your pretty ankles with pants that Marilyn made marvelous.

8.
RULE
BREAKERS

Why follow the rules

when you can break them? Go Gstaad with crisp whites in winter, and be Barcelona with cool blacks in summer.

WHITE made
light and bright
in *SUMMER*

In the summer your
bright whites are always
appropriate. Keep them
fresh and oceanside
friendly with sun-
dappled gold tones in
tops and accessories.

WHITE made
warm and cozy
in *WINTER*

When the mercury drops,
pair your white jeans with
icy shimmering sweaters,
curl-up-by-the-fire vests,
drop-dead boots, and
jewel-toned accessories.

BLACK is sexy in SUMMER

Sultry sequined tanks make hot nights even hotter when paired with black jeans. The bag of choice is exotic and bright, adding a splash of color to your evening ensemble.

BLACK is sexy in WINTER

Form follows function with your black winter jeans tucked into knee-high boots to keep out the chill. Add a warm wrap sweater and a colorful, patterned scarf that complements your personal style.

IZZL, A

DON'T

APOLOG

ACCESS

CESSAR

GUESSO

APOLO

GIZE, AC

ORIZE!

IZE DO

GO DAY-GLO

Achieve full wattage with Sprouse neon tights and an even brighter dress; take it downtown with studded patent pumps and a wooden gemstone clutch.

DON'T apologize, ACCESSORIZE!

When it comes to accessories, mix your materials. *Gone are the days of perfectly matching shoes and bags.* Skins pair with studs, patent flirts with lace, precious meets plastic, and gold finally gets to dance with silver.

DO THE MATH

Angles and spangles add up to the perfect 10. Balance a matte geometric stocking with gravity-defying stilettos; circular baubles soften the edge.

THESE BOOTS ARE MADE FOR WALKING

A textured leather boot goes plastic fantastic with Lucite bangles; an oversized geode ring brings the oversized leather satchel down to earth.

STUDS ARE RIVETING

Punk meets Paris with a ladylike silhouette, lacy stockings, and pedal-to-the-metal embellishments. The updated spectator is dangerous instead of dainty, and burnished snakeskin adds shimmer.

MAINTE

NANCE

9.
BEHIND THE
SEAMS

Want to know what it's like to be an insider? It's about paying attention to the seams as well as the dress, the construction as well as the embellishments, the architectural foundations as well as the finished product. It's understanding that practical makes perfect: looking great isn't just about nuance and inspiration, it's about wearing the right bra, replacing lost buttons, and eradicating the evidence of last night's spaghetti on your favorite white cardi.

PRACTICAL MAKES PERFECT

Sometimes, the quickest way to get a job done is to roll up your sleeves and DIY. But the best way might involve asking a professional for help! In this chapter, we'll cover what you need to know for quick fixes and red alerts.

Get ready to take a peek behind the velvet curtain.

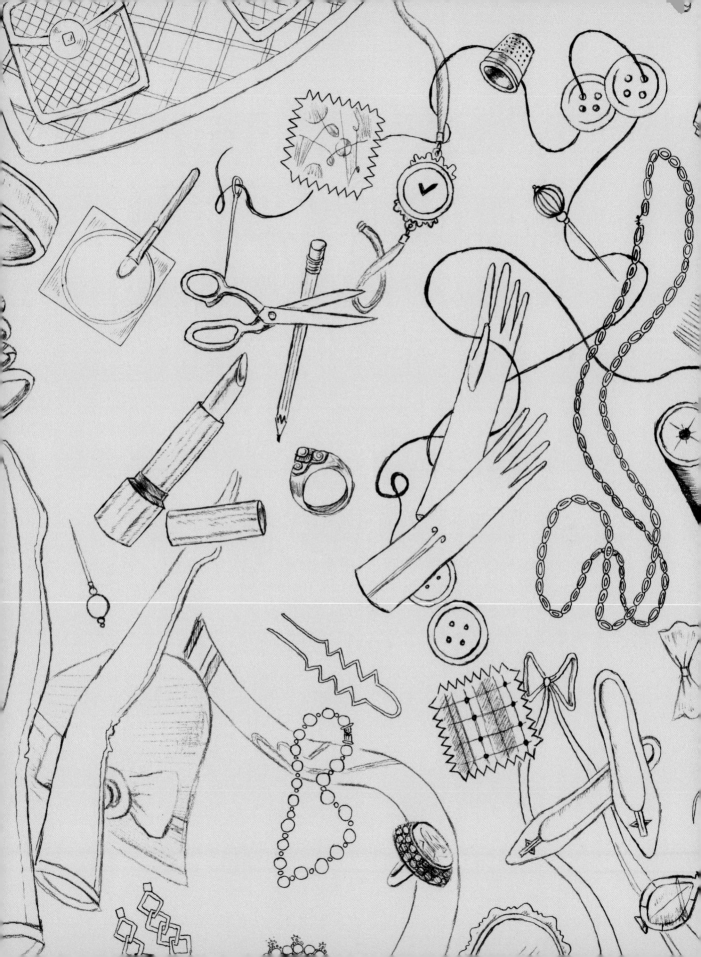

Underarchitecture

engineer the *perfect* underwear *infrastructure*

What you've got on underneath impacts your delectably delicate ensemble, so don't ruin the diaphanous mirage with a blatant display of bra strap or panty line. *Whether your desired look is ephemeral, elegant, or edgy, if you construct the right architectural foundation, you'll be halfway there.*

411: Can't find your number or letter? Jump in either direction. A 34A can wear a 32B and a 36B can wear a 34C.

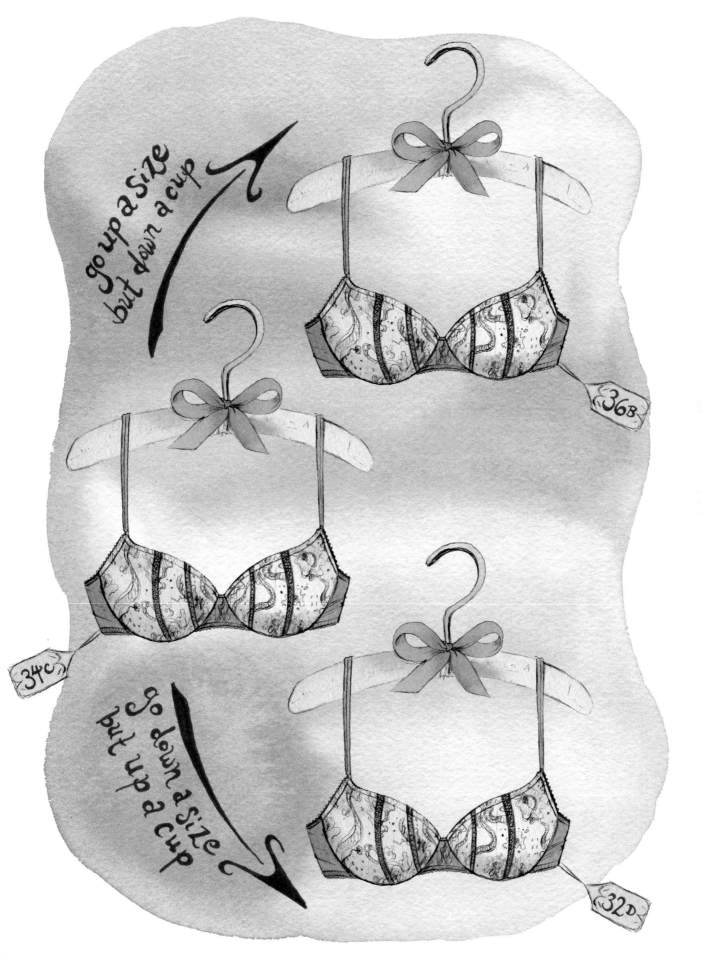

go up a size but down a cup

go down a size but up a cup

36B

34C

32D

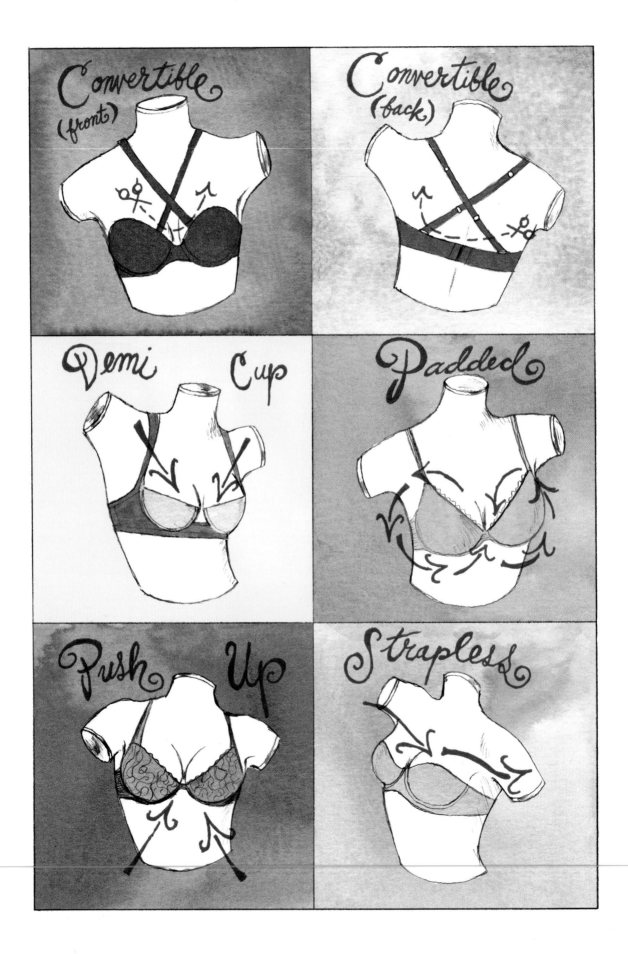

Top Down

Different styles of bras can do wonderful things for a lady's figure but will do nothing at all—or worse—if the fit isn't right. Pop by a local lingerie store, or see if the saleswomen at Victoria's Secret will help you decipher your proper bust and cup size. She'll probably recommend a style to give you killer cleavage and a bit of moral support as well!

CONVERTIBLE
As all-American as Barbie's Dream Car. This wonderful contraption goes three ways without a trace of chagrin, from your traditional over-the-shoulder boulder holder to the racier racerback to the perfect halter (and sometimes, even strapless). Everyone should own a pair: one in black and one in nude.

DEMI
Cut low for when your top is, too.

PADDED
For the girl who sometimes wishes she had a little more in general. Also amazing if you need to fill out a constructed top that is a bit too roomy.

PUSH-UP
For the girl who sometimes wishes she had a little more in the way of cleavage. Also ideal for enhancing an already dangerous silhouette.

SEAMLESS
A.K.A. THE T-SHIRT BRA
Not quite padded but with an extra layer of material so you can wear a thin shirt in a cold room without ever having to cross your arms.

STRAPLESS
Bare shoulders are especially enticing on a balmy evening; keep straps a no-show by going without.

411: Full coverage: if you're a bigger-bosomed girl who likes people to look you in the eye, opt for a modest bra with more support.

411: If you really must increase your bust, there are several nonsurgical, temporary options that are often used in photo shoots. Most lingerie shops carry a line of silicone bra inserts that add instant lift and volume with a natural look. These range in size from "cookies" to "cutlets"; ask a salesperson if you aren't sure which is right for you.

411: The small triangles that come inside most bikini tops are a useful grab for everyday styling needs. They are dynamite underneath halters, silk camis, or any top that is worn without a bra. This padding gives you lineless protection against nipple flare-ups; just apply directly over breasts with a bit of fashion fix (a.k.a. Top Stick; more on this amazing double-sided tape on page 198).

Bottoms Up!

The thong song has been a top-40 favorite but isn't always the best tune. Let these underpinnings make you feel like a contemporary classic as well as a dance-floor diva. Sculpt, slim, and be discreet.

411: VPL (visible panty line) is not an option. Go seamless to avoid unseemly situations.

411: Be beach-blanket bingo with a bikini bottom that lengthens legs and slims waists.

411: Be Brazilian with a thong. South American supermodels do it and so should you—as long as it doesn't ride above the waistline.

SPANX
Not your grandmother's girdle. Spanx are the modern girl's answer to the asphyxiating, curve-adorning corset. Like airbrushing your outfit, these body shapers make you look slim and smooth without your ever having to suck in your breath. They come in a range of lengths and styles, from slips to bicycle shorts and even hose, so no matter what you're wearing, there are no more excuses for errant lumps or bumps.

BIKINI
Neat and sweet, this classic style is just as cute without pants as with.

THONG
The purpose of a thong is to avoid VPL, not create more. If the people around you can see London, France, and your underpants, something is not okay. Pull down your shirt.

BOY SHORT
Functional in cotton, a little sexier in lace, the boy short makes you look every inch a girl.

SEAMLESS
Hate having a perma-wedgie? Seamless panties give you the flawless line of a thong, no strings attached.

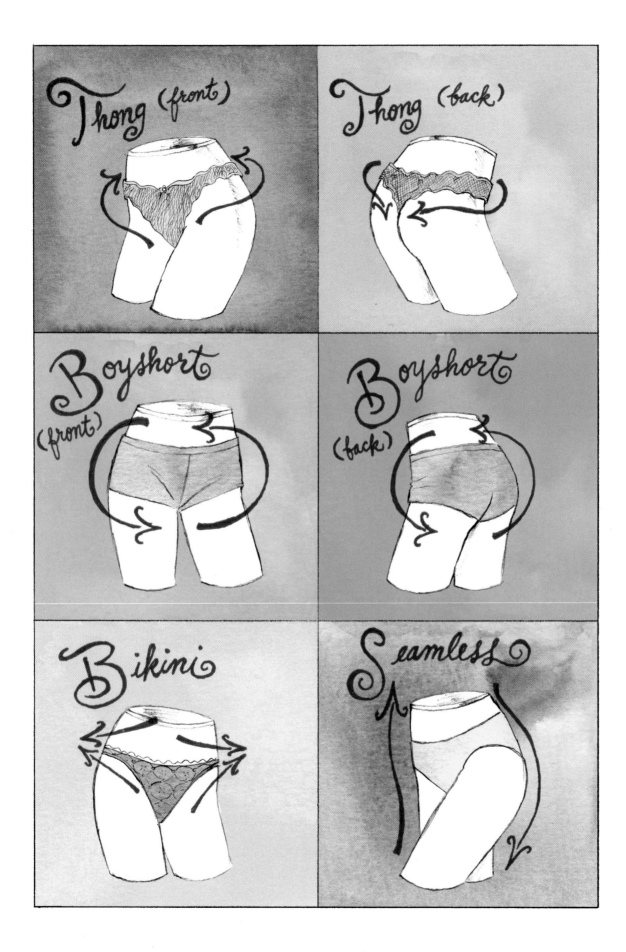

Styling Kit

Dropped your hem? Spilled your milk? Use our handy go-to guide to set up your stock of clothing first aid so you'll be 911-ready no matter what the 411.

411: Wet Ones are a key travel companion, too—not only for sanitizing your hands, but also as a gentle makeup remover that the pros use on the set all the time.

"OUT, DAMNED SPOT!"

You might not be as disturbed as Lady Macbeth, but mysterious spots and stains can be upsetting for anybody. For a story with a happier ending, here are some secret weapons to help you deal with those unintentional splashes and dribbles. Fortunately, you probably already have many of the products I recommend.

TALC (NOT BABY POWDER)
FUNCTION: Gets rid of grease and oil-based stains (like lipstick and food).
FOR: Nonwashables (silks and silk blends, including most knitwear).
HOW TO: Apply generously to spot and let sit for at least an hour or longer. Remove excess gently with a makeup brush or a paper towel, and get the item to the cleaner when the party's over.

DAWN DISHWASHING LIQUID
FUNCTION: Gets rid of grease and oil-based stains (like lipstick and food).
FOR: Washable fabrics (check the label).
HOW TO: Spot-treat the stained area, let it rest for an hour, and then just machine wash the item normally.

WET ONES, ORIGINAL FORMULA
FUNCTION: Instant, on-the-spot spot removal for all your clothing.
FOR: Dried food stains and fresh stains like coffee, tea, wine, and makeup.
HOW TO: Simply pat the stain gently with a fresh Wet One.

GAL PAL DEODORANT REMOVAL PADS
FUNCTION: Gets rid of unsightly and menacing deodorant stains.
FOR: Washable and nonwashable garments with deodorant residue.
HOW TO: Rub against stain, and get those nasty smudges out for good. (You can order these online.)

DRYER SHEETS
FUNCTION: A quick clothing refresher.
FOR: Dry-clean-only garments with a trace of mustiness, whether you've worn them yesterday or not for a while (and need to right now!).
HOW TO: Set your dryer on low heat, toss a scented sheet in along with your garment, and give it a one-minute whirl for a fresh, breezy lift.

FASHION R~X~

MALADY: Any sewing emergency

PRESCRIPTION: Small prefab sewing kit

WHAT IT IS: Miniature set of needles, buttons, threader, small scissors, hook-and-eye kit, snaps, and tape measure that will give you big value for a small price!

THE OPERATION: Catch a hem, replace a button, save a strap

MALADY: Dropped hem on your magenta wool skirt, a loose button on that brilliant yellow cotton chemise, a dangling dress strap on that emerald green silk number

PRESCRIPTION: The rainbow braid

WHAT IT IS: A braid made up of every color thread you might need for a quick repair

THE OPERATION: Give the problem a quick stitch with a piece of thread from this must-have essential for every stylist, a little-known, big-deal treasure. Just choose your color and slip your thread out. Magic!

MALADY: Pills and pulls on your heavy sweaters or coats

PRESCRIPTION: Sweater shaver

WHAT IT IS: An easy-to-use, impossible-to-mess-up-with little electric shaver that whirs away the wear and tear

THE OPERATION: Give your garment a close shave and make it look years younger with the sweater shaver. It's like a quick needle-free face-lift for your sweaters and coats. Repeat as needed.

MALADY: An extra coating of fur

PRESCRIPTION: Lint roller

WHAT IT IS: A brilliant use of masking tape as an indispensable, simple-to-use tool

THE OPERATION: Make sure to give your clothes the once-over before you leave the house—especially if you have pets!

MALADY: Plunging neckline, straying collar, loose hem

PRESCRIPTION: Top Stick Fashion-Fix (double-sided tape)

WHAT IT IS: Sticky on both sides, this skin-safe tape is a user-friendly product and a well-guarded stylist secret that is readily available at most drugstores, specialty lingerie shops, and beauty-supply stores

THE OPERATION: Use directly on skin to hold plunging necklines in place, make collars lay the way you want them to, or catch a loose hem at the last minute.

HAPPILY EVER AFTER

Once upon a time you dreamed of being the belle of the ball. But your gown was a mess, and the duke didn't call. You thought you required a fairy godmother, but all you needed was a charming prince to give you some hope and show you the ropes.

With a wave of your wand and a click of your heels, you whipped your closet into shape. You got inspired. You mixed, matched, hemmed, and cobbled, and made room for a fabulous, fashionable future.

Welcome to the world of style, which is 20 percent fashion, 80 percent confidence. You now have both; you know what you like, and you know what likes you back. So go forth and prosper . . . and live happily ever after.

THE END

xoxo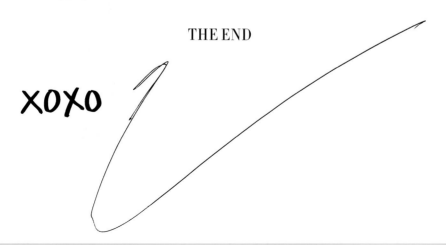

Acknowledgments

A *grand merci* to my family and friends, who push me, inspire me, and support me unconditionally; without you none of this would have been possible.

Thanks to Brian Boyce, my art director of choice; Tonya Huskey, my pro producer, efficient assistant, and BFF; Derek Marks, whose marks have made me proud; Bumper, for *pullin' up to the bumper* and capturing my vision; David Chernis, for helping him make it happen; Marcus Siriotis, for his fine-tuning; my justice league of super-wonder girls: Sami Rattner, Brittany Griffin, Colleen Ehrlich, Lisa Tobias, and Shannon Lumpkin; Rebecca Oliver, the best book agent ever! Period! Jonathan Silverman, for introducing me to Becka and suggesting that I make a book; the Bowery Hotel, Drive-In Studios, Peter at Mascot Studio, Eclectic Encore, Duo, Marie Saeki/MS PR, Erica Baum, Dispatch Bureau, Michael Moreno, and Angela Dicarlo; John Henry, for locating my locations. Who could forget all the lovely ladies at Clarkson Potter, especially Doris Cooper and Aliza Fogelson, Lauren Shakely, Marysarah Quinn, Jane Treuhaft, Stephanie Huntwork, Jill Browning, Donna Passannante, Angelin Borsics, Amy Boorstein, Tricia Wygal, and their dapper Dan, Derek Gullino, for taking such care and actually caring. Leighton Meester, for a foreword that made me misty; Stephanie Savage, for her encouragement, talent, and enthusiasm; the delicious Sandra Bark, for harnessing my unbridled dialogue into witty eloquence; and, of course, my favorite supermodel, Humphrey!

Resources

32: **JEANS:** *Zara;* visit www.zara.com for store locations
SHOES: *Jimmy Choo;* www.jimmy choo.com, Saks Fifth Avenue and Bergdorf Goodman locations

39: **JEANS:** *Jordache;* www.jordache.com, Walmart locations

40: **JEANS:** *J.Brand;* www.jbrandjeans.com, www.revolveclothing.com, Barneys NY and Saks Fifth Avenue locations

41: **JEANS:** *7 for All Mankind;* www.7for allmankind.com, www.revolve clothing.com, Barneys NY locations

42: **JEANS:** *7 for All Mankind;* www.7for allmankind.com, www.revolve clothing.com, Barneys NY locations

43: **JEANS:** *J.Brand;* www.jbrandjeans.com, www.revolveclothing.com, Barneys NY and Saks Fifth Avenue locations

51: **SWEATER:** *Club Monaco;* visit www.club monaco.com for store locations

52: **COWL NECK:** *Autumn Cashmere;* www.revolveclothing.com, Bergdorf Goodman and Neiman Marcus locations; visit www.autumncashmere.com for other retailers
LACE STITCH SWEATER: *Pierrot;* www.voilabypierrot.com

53: **V-NECK SWEATER:** J. Crew, www.jcrew.com
CREW NECK: *Iris Singer,* www.singer22.com

55: **CARDIGAN:** *Zara;* visit www.zara.com for store locations

56: **RED CARDIGAN:** *Brook Brothers;* visit www.BrooksBrothers.com for store locations
STRIPED SWEATER: *Joie;* Saks Fifth Avenue and Bloomingdale's locations; visit www.joie.com for other retailers

57: **RETRO CARDIGAN:** *Top Shop;* www.topshop.com or Top Shop NY, 478 Broadway, New York, NY, (212) 966-9555

EMBELLISHED CARDIGAN: *L.A.M.B.;* www.shopbop.com, Saks Fifth Avenue and Nordstrom locations

60: **OFFICE DRESS:** *Diane von Furstenberg;* www.DVF.com, Barneys NY, Saks Fifth Avenue and Bloomingdale's locations

61: **WEEKEND DRESS:** *Thread Social;* http://social.threaddesign.com, www.shopbop.com, and Intermix store locations

62: **DATE DRESS:** *Alice + Olivia;* www.aliceandolivia.com for boutique locations, Saks Fifth Avenue, Bloomingdale's, and Nordstrom locations

63: **BLACK-TIE DRESS:** *Jil Sander,* 818 Madison Avenue, New York, NY, (212) 838-6100 and Barneys NY locations

64: **OFFICE DRESS:** *Catherine Malandrino;* www.catherinemalandrino.com for locations and Saks Fifth Avenue locations
WEEKEND DRESS: *Top Shop,* www.topshop.com or Top Shop, NY, 478 Broadway, New York, NY, (212) 966-9555

65: **DATE DRESS:** *Black Halo;* visit www.blackhalo.com for online shopping and store locations
BLACK-TIE DRESS: *Kate Moss for Top Shop;* www.topshop.com or Top Shop, NY, 478 Broadway, New York, NY, (212) 966-9555

67: **SUIT:** *Rag & Bone;* www.rag-bone.com for store locations, Barneys NY, Saks Fifth Avenue, and Bergdorf Goodman locations

68: **SCARF:** *Diane von Furstenberg;* www.DVF.com; Barneys NY, Saks Fifth Avenue, and Bloomingdale's locations
BAG: *Nancy Gonzalez;* Bergdorf Goodman and Saks Fifth Avenue locations; visit www.nancy gonzalez.com for other locations

69: **TANK:** *Amen;* www.lindestore.com or www.yoox.com
CLUTCH: *Deepa Gurnani;* www.shopintuition.com
BRACELET: *Alexis Bittar;* Saks Fifth Avenue and Nordstrom locations; visit www.alexisbittar.com for boutique locations

70: **PINK SUIT:** *Pink Tartan;* Saks Fifth Avenue and Bloomingdale's locations; visit www.pinktartan.com for retail locations

71: **JEANS:** *Current Elliott;* www.currentelliott.com, www.revolveclothing.com, Saks Fifth Avenue, and Nordstrom locations
TEE: *James Perse;* www.jamesperse.com, Barneys NY, Bloomingdale's, and Bergdorf Goodman locations

72–73: **BLOUSES:** *Brooks Brothers;* www.BrooksBrothers.com for store locations

74: **BAG:** *Bodhi;* http://shop.bodhibags.net and www.ebags.com
SHOES: *Pour la Victoire;* www.piper lime.com and Bloomingdale's locations
GLASSES: *Selima Optique;* visit www.selimaoptique.com for shopping and store locations
SCARF: *Hayden Harnette;* visit www.haydenharnett.com for shopping and store locations
EARRINGS: *Top Shop;* www.topshop.com or Top Shop NY, 478 Broadway, New York, NY, (212) 966-9555

75: **BAG:** *Bodhi;* http://shop.bodhibags.net and www.ebags.com
SHOES: *Marc Jacobs,* 163 Mercer Street, New York, NY 10012 and Barneys NY locations
GLASSES: *Selima Optique;* visit www.selimaoptique.com for shopping and store locations
HEADBAND: *Cara Coutoure;* www.shopstyle.com
SCARF: *Polo Ralph Lauren;* www.ralph lauren.com, Bloomingdale's and Saks Fifth Avenue locations

76: **BAG:** *B E & D;* www.beandd.com and Neiman Marcus locations
BOOTS: *Maxx Studio;* Bloomingdale's, Lord & Taylor, and Macy's locations
GLASSES: *Selima Optique;* visit www.selimaoptique.com for shopping and store locations
CLUTCH: *Moyna;* www.moynabags.com, Bergdorf Goodman, Henri Bendel, and Lord & Taylor locations
BRACELETS (RIGHT): *Swarovski;* visit www.swarovski.com for shopping and boutique locations; **(LEFT)** *Alexis Bittar;* www.alexisbittar.com for boutique locations, Saks Fifth Avenue and Nordstrom locations
BROOCH: *Alexis Bittar;* www.alexis bittar.com for boutique locations, Saks Fifth Avenue and Nordstrom locations

77: **BAG:** *Bodi;* http://shop.bodhibags.net and www.ebags.com
SHOES: *D & G;* visit www.dolce gabbana.com for shopping and store locations
BRACELET: *Earrings Plaza;* 1263 Broadway, New York, NY 10001, (212) 685-5666
EARRINGS: *Alexis Bittar;* www.alexis bittar.com for boutique locations, Saks Fifth Avenue and Nordstrom locations
RING: *Swarovski;* visit www.swarovski .com for shopping and boutique locations

80: **COAT:** *Burberry;* www.burberryusa online.com, Saks Fifth Avenue, Bergdorf Goodman, and Barneys NY locations
BAG: *Bottega Veneta;* www.bottegaveneta.com; Bergdorf Goodman locations
SUNGLASSES: *Selima Optique;* visit www.selimaoptique.com for shopping and store locations

81: **COAT:** *Elie Tahari;* Saks Fifth Avenue, Nordstrom; visit www.elietahari.com for other store locations
BAG: *Lockheart;* Nordstrom locations; Contact Pam Gregorio at (800) 783-2160 x2 or info@lockheart.com for further information

82: **DRESS:** *ADAM;* www.revolve clothing.com, Saks Fifth Avenue locations; visit www.shopadam.com for shopping and store locations
SUNGLASSES: *Selima Optique;* visit www.selimaoptique.com for shopping and store locations
SHOES: *Delman;* http://delmanshoes .com, http://couture.zappos.com, Neiman Marcus and Bergdorf Goodman locations

83: **ALL ITEMS:** *Charlotte Russe;* visit www.charlotterusse.com for online shopping and store locations

84: **ALL ITEMS:** *Charlotte Russe;* visit www.charlotterusse.com for online shopping and store locations

85: **JEANS:** *Current Elliott;* www.current elliott.com, www.revolveclothing .com, Saks Fifth Avenue and Nordstrom locations
TOP: *Alice + Olivia;* www.aliceand olivia.com for boutique locations, Saks Fifth Avenue, Bloomingdale's, and Nordstrom locations
SHOES: *Mistique;* www.zappos.com and www.piperlime.com

94: **PINK SHOE:** *Alexander McQueen;* www.alexandermcqueen.com, www.zappos.com, and Saks Fifth Avenue locations

111: **HAT:** *Louise Green;* www.louisegreen.com
TOP: *Diane von Furstenberg;* www.DVF.com, Barneys NY, Saks Fifth Avenue, and Bloomingdale's locations
DRESS: *Lanvin;* Bergdorf Goodman and Barneys NY locations
BAG: *Nancy Gonzalez;* Bergdorf Goodman and Saks Fifth Avenue locations; visit www.nancy gonzalez.com for other locations

114–15: **CAFTAN:** *Milly;* www.shopbop.com, Saks Fifth Avenue and Bergdorf Goodman locations
GLASSES: *Selima Optique;* visit www.selimaoptique.com for shopping and store locations
HEAD SCARF: *Hayden Harnette;* visit www.haydenharnett.com for shopping and store locations

118: **HAT:** *Louise Green;* www.louisegreen.com
TOP: *Hanii Y;* www.revolve clothing.com, Saks Fifth Avenue and Bloomingdale's locations
SWEATER: *Dries van Noten;* Barneys NY and Bergdorf Goodman locations

122: **NECKLACE:** *Stephen Dweck;* www.stephendweck.com for online shopping; Bergdorf Goodman and Saks Fifth Avenue locations
BAG: *Chanel;* visit www.chanel.com for boutique locations
VINTAGE DRESS: found at New York Vintage, 117 W. 25th Street, New York, NY 10001, (212) 647-1107

128: **GLASSES:** *Selima Optique;* visit www.selimaoptique.com for shopping and store locations

129: **NECKLACE:** *Bounkit;* http://shop.boun kit.com, www.marissacollections.com, and www.vivre.com
EARRINGS: *Miguel Ases;* www.miguel ases.com and www.maxandchloe.com

130: **HATS:** *Kate Spade;* www.katespade.com and Bloomingdale's locations

131: **HEADBANDS:** *L. Erickson;* www.franceluxe.com

139: **DRESS:** *Burberry;* www.burberryusa online.com, Saks Fifth Avenue, Bergdorf Goodman, and Barneys NY locations

143: **HAT:** *J. Lamont;* Barneys NY, Henri Bendel, and Fred Segal locations
TOP: *Bally;* www.bally.com
NECKLACE (LONG): *Bettina Louise;* call (845) 534-8292 for ordering information
NECKLACE (SHORT): *Gabriela De La Vega;* www.gabrieladelavega.com
SKIRT: *Gregory Parkinson;* Gregory Parkinson, 117 West 9th Street, #1005, Los Angeles, CA 90015, (213) 622-0722 or contact shop@gregoryparkinson .com; Barneys NY locations

147: **JACKET:** *Gucci;* visit www.gucci.com for shopping and store locations
PANTS: *The Row;* Barneys NY and Bergdorf Goodman locations
BOOTS: *Ralph Lauren;* www.ralph lauren.com or DSW locations

151: **DRESS:** *Diane von Furstenberg;*
www.DVF.com, Barneys NY, Saks
Fifth Avenue, and Bloomingdale's
locations

155: **DRESS:** vintage *Oscar de la Renta;* New
York Vintage, 117 W. 25th Street, New
York, NY 10001, (212) 647-1107
SCARF: *Oscar de la Renta;*
www.oscardelarenta.com for shopping
and store locations

163: **PURPLE SKIRT:** *Helene Berman;*
Nordstrom locations

164: **PLEATED SKIRT:** *Surface to Air;*
www.surface2airparis.com and
Barneys NY
PLAID SKIRT: *L.A.M.B.;* www.shop
bop.com, Saks Fifth Avenue and
Nordstrom locations

165: **ENVELOPE SKIRT:** *Rag & Bone;*
Barneys NY, Saks Fifth Avenue, and
Bergdorf Goodman locations; visit
www.rag-bone.com for store locations
PENCIL SKIRT: *Catherine Malandrino;*
Saks Fifth Avenue locations; visit
www.catherinemalandrino.com for
shopping and boutique locations

167: **YELLOW CARDIGAN:** *Joie;* Saks Fifth
Avenue and Bloomingdale's locations;
visit www.joie.com for other retailers

168: **(LEFT) SWEATER VEST:** *Charles Nolan;*
30 Gansevoort Street, New York, NY
10014, (888) 99-NOLAN,
www.shopcharlesnolan.com
BLOUSE: *Brooks Brothers;* www.Brooks
Brothers.com for store locations
(RIGHT) TOP: *Theory;* www.theory
.com, Barneys NY, Saks Fifth Avenue,
and Bloomingdale's locations
JACKET: *Isli;* www.shopbop.com and
Bloomingdale's locations

169: **(LEFT) TOP:** *Theory;* www.theory
.com, Barneys NY, Saks Fifth Avenue,
and Bloomingdale's locations
(RIGHT) TOP: *Cake;* www.couture
candy.com and http://cakecouture.net
JACKET: *Doma;* www.doma-leather
.com and Bloomingdale's locations

171: **WHITE PANTS:** *RED Valentino;*
www.valentino.com, Saks Fifth
Avenue and Intermix locations

172: **PINSTRIPE PANTS:** *Theory;*
www.theory.com, Barneys NY, Saks
Fifth Avenue, and Bloomingdale's
locations
TWEED PANTS: *Tory Burch;* Saks Fifth
Avenue and Bergdorf Goodman
locations; visit www.toryburch.com
for other store and boutique locations

173: **GREEN PANTS:** *Barbara Tfank;* Saks Fifth
Avenue locations
ORANGE PANTS: *Piazza Sempione;*
Barneys NY locations; visit
www.piazzasempione.com for other
store locations

174-75: **ALL JEWELRY:** *Swarovski;* visit
www.swarovski.com for shopping and
boutique locations

176: **JEANS:** *J.Brand;* www.jbrandjeans.com,
www.revolveclothing.com, Barneys
NY and Saks Fifth Avenue locations
TOP: *Burberry;*
www.burberryusaonline.com, Saks
Fifth Avenue, Bergdorf Goodman, and
Barneys NY locations
BAG: *B E & D;* www.beandd.com and
Neiman Marcus locations

177: **SWEATER:** *DKNY;* Macy's locations;
visit www.dkny.com for other
shopping and store locations
VEST: *Gryphon;* www.shopbop
.com, Saks Fifth Avenue, Bergdorf
Goodman, and Intermix locations
BOOTS: Ralph Lauren; www.ralph
lauren.com, Bloomingdale's and Saks
Fifth Avenue locations
BAG: Patricia Carter Collection;
www.pcartercollections.com

178: **JEANS:** *J.Brand;* www.jbrandjeans.com,
www.revolveclothing.com, Barneys
NY and Saks Fifth Avenue locations
TANK: *3.1 Phillip Lim;* Barneys NY,
Bergdorf Goodman, Neiman Marcus,
and Nordstrom locations

179: **JEANS:** *J.Brand;* www.jbrandjeans.com,
www.revolveclothing.com, Barneys
NY and Saks Fifth Avenue locations
BOOTS: *Delman;* http://delman
shoes.com, http://couture.zappos
.com, Neiman Marcus and Bergdorf
Goodman locations
BAG: *Kotur;* visit www.koturltd.com
for store locations
SWEATER: *Hessnatur;* visit http://us.hess
natur.com for online shopping

182: **DRESS:** *Marc Jacobs;* 163 Mercer Street,
New York, NY 10012; Barneys NY
locations
SHOES: *Giuseppe Zanotti;* Barneys
NY, Saks Fifth Avenue, and Bergdorf
Goodman locations; visit
www.giuseppe-zanotti-design.com
for boutique locations
BAG: *Devi Kroell;*
www.devikroell.com, Barneys NY and
Jeffrey's locations
BRACELETS (BLUE AND GOLD): *CCSkye;*
www.ccskye.com, Bloomingdale's,
Neiman Marcus, Nordstrom, and Saks
Fifth Avenue locations
BRACELETS (GOLD): *Alexis Bittar;*
www.alexisbittar.com for boutique
locations; Saks Fifth Avenue and
Nordstrom locations

183: **DRESS:** *Diane von Furstenberg;*
www.DVF.com; Barneys NY,
Bloomingdale's, and Saks Fifth Avenue
locations
SHOES: *Armani;*
www.giorgioarmani.com
RING: *Stephen Dweck;* www.stephen
dweck.com, Bergdorf Goodman and
Saks Fifth Avenue locations
BRACELET (SNAKE SKIN): *Kara
Ross;* Bergdorf Goodman and
Bloomingdale's locations; visit
www.kararossny.com for other stores
and online shopping
BRACELET (BLUE STONE): *Stephen
Dweck;* Bergdorf Goodman and Saks
Fifth Avenue locations; visit
www.stephendweck.com for online
shopping
BRACELET (GOLD BUCKLE): *CC Skye;*
www.ccskye.com; Bloomingdale's,
Neiman Marcus, Nordstrom, and Saks
Fifth Avenue locations
BRACELET (GOLD BRAIDED): *Eva New
York;* 227 Mulberry Street, #3, New
York, NY 10012, (212) 925-3208
BAG: *Surly Girl;*
www.shopsurlygirl.com

184: **BOOTS:** *Fendi;* visit www.fendi.com for
boutique locations; Bloomingdale's,
Neiman Marcus, and Saks Fifth Avenue
locations
**BRACELETS (BRONZE/SILVER; PURPLE;
GOLD):** *Alexis Bittar;*
www.alexisbittar.com for boutique
locations; Nordstrom and Saks Fifth
Avenue locations

BRACELET (MULTISTONE): *Bounkit;*
http://shop.bounkit.com,
www.marissacollections.com, and
www.vivre.com
BAG: *Linea Pelle;* www.lpcollection.com
and www.bluefly.com

185: **DRESS:** *Diane von Furstenberg;*
www.DVF.com, Barneys NY,
Bloomingdale's, and Saks Fifth Avenue
locations
BAG: *Surly Girl;*
www.shopsurlygirl.com

SHOES: *Giuseppe Zanotti;* visit
www.giuseppe-zanotti-design.com
for boutique locations; Barneys NY,
Bergdorf Goodman, and Saks Fifth
Avenue locations
RING: *CC Skye;* www.ccskye.com,
Bloomingdale's, Neiman Marcus,
Nordstrom, and Saks Fifth Avenue
locations
BRACELET (CHARM): *Stephen Dweck;*
shop online at www.stephen
dweck.com, Bergdorf Goodman and
Saks Fifth Avenue locations

BRACELET (BLACK BANGLE): *Prada;*
Bergdorf Goodman and Saks Fifth
Avenue locations
BRACELET (GOLD LINK): *CC Skye;*
www.ccskye.com, Bloomingdale's,
Neiman Marcus, Nordstrom, and Saks
Fifth Avenue locations
TIGHTS: *Falke;* www.shopbop.com and
www.barenecessities.com

Credits

Photography by Bumper Photography, with the exception of pages 4, 12, 78, 96–97, 156–157, courtesy of the author; page 7 by Shannon Lumpkin; pages 16–17, 32–33, 48–49, 51, 52–53, 55, 56–57, 60–61, 62–63, 64–65, 72–73, 74–75, 76–77, 99, 174–75, 186–87, 196 by David Chernis Photography; page 104, GOSSIP GIRL © Warner Bros. Entertainment Inc., all rights reserved; and page 159 by Erica Baum, *Shampoo*, 2008.

Lettering by Brian Lee Boyce

Illustrations by Derek Marks

Index

accessories
  See also bags; jewelry; sunglasses
  face-framing, 126–31
  mixing, 182–85
  signature pieces, 78–79
  types of occasions, 74–77
  using color, 126–31
A-line skirts, 27
apple (O-frame) body type, 18, 20
autumn, and color, 109, 118–21

bags, 81, 182–85
bandage dress, 58–59
Basics, shopping list, 30
black, comparing summer and winter wear, 178, 179
black dresses, 60–63
black-tie events, 63, 65, 76
blouses. *See* chemise tops
boatneck tops, 23
body types. *See* figure types
boot-cut jeans, 41
boyfriend cardigans, 55, 167
bras, 191, 192–93

cable-knit sweaters, 51, 53
capri pants, 43, 173
cardigan sweaters, 51, 54–57, 167, 169
carrot (T-frame) body type, 18, 20
cashmere sweaters, 50–53, 169
Chanel, Coco, 98
chemise tops, 23, 72–73, 168
cigarette pants, 24, 173
circle skirts, 26
Classic archetype, 134, 136–39
closets, purging, 86–91
coats, 80–81
colors
  identifying your seasonal palette, 108–25
  using as inspiration, 106
cowl-neck sweaters, 52
crew-neck tops, 23, 53

dates, dressing for, 62, 65, 69, 77
double-sided tape, 198

Dramatic archetype, 135, 148–51
dresses
  black, 59, 60–63
  for black-tie events, 63, 65
  for dates, 62, 65
  lengths, 28–29
  for office, 60, 64
  for weekends, 61, 64
Dress-up Essentials, 62–73

Eclectic archetype, 134, 140–43
embellished cardigans, 57, 169
Everyday Basic Essentials, 34–57

fashion archetypes, 132–55
figure types
  best pants for, 24–25
  best skirts for, 26–27
  best tops for, 22–23
  defined, 20
  determining, 20–21
  illustrated, 18–19
  taking measurements, 21
flare-bottom pants, 25
framing your face, 126–31

halter tops, 22
hats, to frame face, 130
hemlines, length guide, 28–29

investment purchases
  vs. wardrobe fillers, 82–85
  what to spend money on, 80, 81

jackets, 168, 169
  See also coats; suits; sweaters
jeans
  back pockets, 36–37
  fitting, 34–35
  and style, 38–43
jewelry, 78–79, 129, 182–85

lacy stitch sweaters, 52, 168
layering, 160–73
Leger, Herve, 58–59

maintenance. *See* repair and maintenance

measurements, to determine body type, 21
men's and boy's T-shirts, 47, 48
miniskirts, 27, 163, 164
Natural archetype, 134, 144–47

office, dressing for, 60, 64, 67, 68, 70, 75

panties, 194–95
pants
  for body types, 24–25
  jeans, 32–43
  and style, 170–73
pear (A-frame) body type, 19, 20
pencil skirts, 27, 165
pleated skirts, 26, 163, 164
pockets, on jeans, 36–37
purses, 81, 182–85

repair and maintenance
  caring for shoes, 94–95
  first-aid for clothes, 196–99
  hiring tailors, 92–93
Romantic archetype, 135, 152–55

shirts, 72–73, 168
  See also T-shirts
shoes
  maintaining, 94–95
  mixing accessories, 182–85
shorts, 24
signature pieces, 78–79
skinny jeans, 40
skirts
  See also dresses
  for body types, 26–27
  lengths, 28–29
  and style, 162–65
Spanx, 194
spring, and color, 108, 110–13
stain removal, 197
straight-leg pants, 25, 39
stringbean (I-frame) body type, 19, 20
style
  elements, 158–73
  finding one's own, 98–105

in jeans, 38–43
in pants, 170–73
in skirts, 162–65
in tops, 166–69
styling kit, 196–99
stylist
  art of, 13, 105, 106
  becoming your own, 102–3
  thinking like one, 98, 105
suits
  office and beyond, 66–71
  shirts for, 72–73
summer, and color, 108, 114–17, 176, 178
sunglasses, 81, 128
sweaters
  See also jackets
  cable-knit, 51, 53
  cardigan, 51, 54–57, 167, 169
  cashmere, 50–53, 169
  maintenance, shaving, 198

T-shirts, 46–49
tailors, hiring, 92–93
Top Stick, 198
tops
  See also jackets
  for body types, 22–23
  chemise-type, 23, 72–73, 168
  layering, 166–69
  shirts for suits, 72–73, 168
  and style, 166–69
  sweaters, 50–57, 167, 169
  T-shirts, 46–49
trench coat, 80
trousers, 24, 25, 42, 171
tunic cardigan sweater, 56

underwear, 190–95

V-neck tops, 22, 53

weekend dressing, 61, 64, 71, 74
white, comparing summer and winter wear, 176, 177
winter, and color, 109, 121–25, 177, 179

About the Author

Eric Daman was studying French literature at the Sorbonne when he was discovered by photographer Steven Meisel. His modeling career led him to the realization that his true love was styling, and a move to New York City launched his styling career. Today, Eric is heralded as one of the seven influencers "who could change everything about the way we look" (*Allure,* March 2009).

From television to magazines to the big screen, Eric Daman is synonymous with style. His work as the costume designer for the WB's hit show *Gossip Girl* was lauded on the cover of the *New York Times* and his work as assistant designer to Patricia Field on *Sex and the City* won him an Emmy. Eric has designed costumes for everyone from Leighton Meester and Blake Lively to Kim Basinger, Hayden Panettiere, and Isabella Rossellini. He is the Creative Consultant for Charlotte Russe and lives in New York City.

You Know You Want It: Style-Inspiration-Confidence is his first book.

DE TOUF
SE BEY
JR OW
VN MU
MUSE